Autobiography as *Burla*
in the *Guzmán de Alfarache*

Autobiography as *Burla* in the *Guzmán de Alfarache*

Nina Cox Davis

Lewisburg
Bucknell University Press
London and Toronto: Associated University Presses

© 1991 by Associated University Presses, Inc.

All rights reserved. Authorization to photocopy items for internal or personal use, or the internal or personal use of specific clients, is granted by the copyright owner, provided that a base fee of $10.00, plus eight cents per page, per copy is paid directly to the Copyright Clearance Center, 27 Congress Street, Salem, Massachusetts 01970. [0-8387-5221-7/91 $10.00 + 8¢ pp, pc.]

Associated University Presses
440 Forsgate Drive
Cranbury, NJ 08512

Associated University Presses
25 Sicilian Avenue
London WC1A 2QH, England

Associated University Presses
P.O. Box 39, Clarkson Pstl. Stn.
Mississauga, Ontario
Canada L5J 3X9

The paper used in this publication meets the requirements of the American National Standard for Permanence of Paper for Printed Library Materials Z39.48-1984.

Library of Congress Cataloging-in-Publication Data

Davis, Nina Cox, 1953–
    Autobiography as burla in the Guzmán de Alfarache / Nina Cox Davis.
    p.   cm.
    Includes bibliographical references and index.
    ISBN 0–8387–5221–7 (alk. paper)
    1. Alemán, Mateo, 1547–1614? Aventuras y vida de Guzmán de Alfarache. 2. Wit and humor in literature. 3. Autobiography in literature. I. Title.
PQ6272.Z5D38   1991
863'.3—dc20   91-55272
                                                          CIP

Printed in the United States of America

For Christopher

Contents

Preface	9
Introduction	13
1. The "figure" Guzmán	22
The "inconstant figure of this discourse" 28	
"An accepted courtier" 43	
2. Guzmán's History	61
From Recipient to Author of Jokes 70	
Guzmán, the dupe 70	
Guzmán, the joker: "licensed" versus	
"creative" petty theft 72	
Burlas as Art 79	
Guzmán as jester 81	
Guzmán as comic fool 91	
Guzmán, the Author of His Life 94	
3. Guzmán Tells His Story	108
The Silversmith 112	
The Milanese Merchant 116	
Guzmán's Relatives 121	
Conclusion	129
Notes	132
Bibliography	144
Index	151

Preface

This study, the preliminary step in what I hope will be a broader look at autobiography as *burla* in the Spanish picaresque genre, has evolved through several stages. I am grateful for the criticisms, guidance, and support of a number of persons as it developed. I would like particularly to thank Elias Rivers for his important support early on; Harry Sieber for many constructive criticisms in its initial formulation and since; my colleagues at Washington University for their reading of segments; and the University itself for financial support of the project through a Summer Faculty Research Grant. Last, and most important, I would like to thank my husband, Christopher Dadian, for his tireless contributions of editorial and technical expertise, and for support of a more substantial nature that words do not describe.

Autobiography as *Burla*
in the *Guzmán de Alfarache*

Introduction

Mateo Alemán's *Guzmán de Alfarache*, Part One, was the first Spanish narrative to be referred to by Golden Age readers as the story of a *pícaro*, a term that subsequently came to signify a trickster whose wiles posed a threat to society.[1] The tone and scope of Alemán's fictive autobiography, however, distinguish it sharply from later works of the genre, and have led generations of readers to question both the author's intentions and the relationship of his work to its successors. Characterized by a monumental, commentating discourse that repeatedly frames and bisects the exploits of its narrative history, the *Guzmán* bears the appearance of a serious anomaly whose verbose didacticism was parodied in the mock confessions of *libros de entretenimiento* (jest books) that followed.[2]

Modern readers have examined Alemán's encyclopedic work from many perspectives, in most cases sharing the assumption that "serious," overtly ideological propositions motivated the organization of his fictive narrative. For some, the *Guzmán* is resoundingly monologic, representing in allegorical or verisimilar terms a process of personal spiritual development that conforms with Counterreformation doctrine.[3] For other critics, Alemán's narrative is instead structured on a system of utterances that might be referred to, with Bakhtin's terms, as an inherent dialogism, or heteroglossia. They argue that its narrator espouses the Catholic ideology of late sixteenth-century Spain only to question radically the social effects of its implementation. Guzmán exhibits this "bifronted posture"[4] through a system of poetic enunciation that—these critics assert—betrays his ideological affinities with the heterodox beliefs of *conversos*, as it gives voice to the economic, judicial, and political problems resulting from his society's official struggle against pluralism.[5]

My own study of the *Guzmán de Alfarache* owes much both to recent North American *Guzmán* scholarship and to the work of European sociocritics, as the following pages will demonstrate. In addition, Smith's deconstructive reading of the *Guzmán* in *Writing in the Margin* broaches theoretical questions about narrative and authority that I consider crucial for an understanding of Alemán's autobiographical art as communication. While my views on certain important aspects of the *Guzmán*—its discursive polyvalence and preoccupation with social margination, for example—are clearly in consonance with those of other contemporary critics, this book is dedicated to study of an aspect of Alemán's narrative that has not received due attention: the *burlas*, a broad range of jokes that make up Guzmán's life—that is, the autobiography that substantiates his existence—and their didactic or "serious" function.[6] While routine reference is made in most studies of the work to the narrator's witty deceptions, they have often been accorded the function of peripatetic fictions that do not develop the novel's serious ideological intentions. Only Joly (*La Bourle et son interprétation*) and Rodríguez (*El narrador pícaro*) have considered at length the significance of *burlas* in the structuring of Guzmán's message. Although neither critic's book is dedicated principally to this crucial aspect of communication in Alemán's work, their conclusions call for a major reevaluation of the terms of the *Guzmán*'s didacticism.

These two critics explore important questions raised earlier about the *Guzmán*'s overall seriousness by Chevalier in an article that has not been widely circulated ("*Guzmán de Alfarache* en 1605"). In this study, Chevalier closes a succinct but suggestive review of the abundant popular jocose material in the *Guzmán* with the testimony of several of Alemán's contemporary readers, who themselves referred to the work as an "obra de entretenimiento," "para divertirse" (jest book, for their entertainment) (145–46). Citing her own sources (146) as well as Rico's (from *Novela picaresca*, xc–xciii), Chevalier reminds modern readers that Alemán's Part I was widely known as the "Pícaro." The critic argues (146) "cuando sabemos que el siglo XVII leyó *Don Quijote* como libro de aventuras burlescas, l.. equiparación no indica, por cierto, alto aprecio del valor didáctico de *Guzmán*" [knowing that the seventeenth century read the *Quijote* as a book of burlesque adventures, the comparison certainly does not indicate high estimation of the *Guzmán*'s didactic worth]. Consideration of Chevalier's argument may not, perhaps, necessitate our abandoning notions of the "didactic worth" that is the cornerstone of almost every school of contemporary *Guzmán* criticism. We must, however, reevaluate the terms of the narrative's instruction in light of its *burlas*.

In *La Bourle et son interprétation*, Joly applies the dialectical method of Cros's *Protée et le gueux* to the function of *facétie* or *burlas* (jokes) in sixteenth- and seventeenth-century Spanish literature with picaresque features, including novels of the genre proper, narratives of Cervantes, and dramatic works. Her study traces the process of "defolklorickization" (term from 503–4) through which popular jocose materials are bonded in these literary works with Ciceronian witticisms and incorporated into rhetorical designs that both unmask social aggression as "burlar" (to dupe) and depict its punishment or justice in the culprit's "burlarse" (being him- or herself ridiculed) (2, 10). Joly argues that Alemán was the first author to use the term *burla* in chapter titles (nine of fifty-four, to be exact), making this type of communication the most prominent structuring principle to link the first and second parts (62). Her study, which consists of an extensive, annotated lexicon and a glossary of terms semantically related to *la burla*, with analyses of its function in the development of characters and places of the plots of many literary texts, highlights both Guzmán's *graciosas burlas* (comic jests) in the employ of courtiers and his victimization in *burlas pesadas* (injurious practical jokes) at inns. In the dialectical operations of Alemán's narrative, Joly maintains, the discourse of *burlas* in fact reinforces that which moralizes, through the unexpected lexical allusions in *burlas* to those slated by the author for ridicule as *burladores* (jokers). An example is her analysis (376–77) of terms with which Alemán characterizes the innkeeper in an early episode of Part I as both minister of justice and culprit, with the dual roles of *cuadrillero* (rural policeman) and thief. Although Joly's encyclopedic study limits itself to the lexical analysis and cataloguing of isolated *burlas* from the narrative of Guzmán's personal history, her theoretical paradigm of *burlar/burlarse* has important implications for our consideration of the narrating discourse that calls such *burlas* into play in Alemán's work. For while the preterite of the narrative unfolds upon linguistic polysemia whose function is latently editorial, as Cros and others have shown, the present authorial voice of the work's moralizing discourse readily admits to rhetorical ambiguity that is intended to sway the readers' opinions.

Although he unmasks and criticizes other joker figures within his narrative, Alemán's narrator primarily strives to explain the terms of his own existence and, as Reed argues (*Reader in the Picaresque*, 70–71), to direct the readers' judgments of the communication they read. In the problematic lines that link the opening of Alemán's Part II to Part I, the narrating *pícaro* himself foregrounds caution for readers, that the jokes and pranks of his narrated history serve as instructive prelude to the present-tense communication that he undertakes in relating his story:

> Y si dijeres que hago ascos de mi propio trato, que te lo vendo caro haciéndome de rogar o que hago melindre, pesaráme que lo juzgues a tal. Que, aunque es notoria verdad haber servido siempre a el embajador,

mi señor, de su gracioso, entonces pude, aunque no supe, y, aunque agora supiese, no puedo, porque tienen mucha costa y no todo tiempo es uno. Mas, para que no ignores lo que digo y sepas cuáles eran mis gracias entonces y lo que agora sería necesario para ellas, oye con atención el capítulo siguiente. (II, 1, 1: 44–45)

[And if you say that I turn up my nose at my own behavior, that I sell it to you dearly wanting to be coaxed, or that I feign affectation, it will grieve me that you so judge it. For, although my having always served the ambassador, my lord, as his comic is a well-known fact, then I managed to do so, although I didn't know how, and now, even though I might know how, I cannot, for they (jokes) are costly and times are different. Yet, so that you will not overlook what I say and so that you may know the nature of my jests then and what now would be necessary for them, listen carefully to the following chapter.][7]

As Rodríguez points out (*El narrador pícaro*, 71–92), the narrator thus attributes to himself the potential function of a *gracioso* (entertaining comic) in his role as fictive author. Given the challenge of trying to look good while persuading readers to admire him with the narrative of his wrongs, according to Rodríguez (72), Guzmán attempts to influence readers with an arsenal of rhetorical amplificatory techniques that, in terms of the narrative context, constitute gossip, about both others and himself. In effect, the critic argues (86), the penitent narrator attempts to buy his destinaries' *gracia* (forgiveness) in exchange for *gracias* (witticisms).

Guzmán's literary function—an entertainer whose subservient posture wins reward as it affirms his inferiority to readers—is paired in Rodríguez's schema with three other social roles: galley slave, dealer, and thief. I suggest that the latter three comprise a single discursive function, whose force in the autobiographical narrative counters that of the so-called "gracioso." In contrast with what Maravall ("Relaciones de dependencia," 5, 22 and *Literatura picaresca desde la historia social*, 220–36) has characterized as the socially integrative, often propagandistic drive of the narrative posture that Rodríguez designates as that of the *gracioso*, in his various jobs, the narrator Guzmán also exhibits the transgressive restlessness of the popular joker figure by assuming the guise of various types of social offenders.[8] By placing the enunciation of the *pícaro*'s lifestory itself within a context of social intercourse, Rodríguez's analysis demonstrates the important economy of the communication that Guzmán undertakes in writing his life: the *pícaro* aims to profit from his composition, whether he appropriates his own gain through poetic transgression or receives it in favorable response from readers to his entertainment. However, I would argue for a reduction in the narrator Guzmán's disguise "offices" to two discursive functions—one of a voice that might be termed that of a *juglar discreto* (prudent jester) and one, simultaneously, of an enunciation that might be designated that of a *burlador indiscreto* (impudent joker).

I employ the term *juglar discreto*, rather than Rodríguez's *gracioso*, for a deliberate reason. Usage associates the former with literary composition and courtly patronage, while the latter is a theatrical figure whose antics mollify the *vulgo* (commoners). As the following study will make clear, I believe that the *Guzmán*, like the *Lazarillo*, is structured as a composition implicitly intended by the fictive author, its narrator, for reading and response by fictional social superiors. It is a *caso*, or "case" in the quasi-legal sense, which the general public of real readers is allowed the voyeurism of perusing. The discursive function of *juglar* entails Guzmán's enlightenment and entertainment of fictive and, hence, real readers with the language of the class to which both presumably aspire: that of *discretos*, a prudent elite whose privilege derives—as the following study will demonstrate— either from critical acumen informed by education or from socioeconomic might.[9] Within the framework of the risible account of his own misdeeds, the narrator with critical perspicacity and rhetorical indirection implicates both levels of readers in a common economy of transgression, while positing only the example of his own life—the book we read—as the butt of their laughter and possible derision. The *juglar discreto* (prudent jester), Guzmán, thus serves with his art while affirming the authority of readers to dictate the terms of the relationship that binds them, through their response of judgment and reward. At the same time, in parodying the discourses of their authority—sermonic rhetoric, philosophical logic, legal dictums, religious doctrine, and other specialized, learned lexicons, Guzmán the narrator also functions as a *burlador indiscreto* (impudent joker), a popular trickster figure. By usurping the very discursive systems that define and thus substantiate the privilege of his superiors, and by using them in the context of his own unauthorized bid for figural authority, the narrator effectively questions the privilege that presumed *discretos* have assigned to their own existence.[10] The language that structures the society of his readers is, Alemán's work implies, potentially as arbitrary and ideologically interested in its referentiality as is the *pícaro*'s use of that same language to represent reality through his own eyes.

Without discussing the theoretical implications of the discursive oscillation that they represent, Rodríguez offers through the various authorial *personae* previously cited a complication to the resolution sought by Joly's dialectical analysis of the narrative as a process of *burlar/burlarse*, or joking displayed and then castigated. I must agree with the direction of Rodríguez's analysis, that the function of *burlas* in the *Guzmán*'s structure is more pervasive and complex than that of discrete narrative units dedicated to conveying judgment. The narrative does indeed work to expose the deception and hypocrisy of Guzmán and the world around him. However, its social commentary is conveyed through a narrating discourse whose composition itself simultaneously constitutes *burlas*, designed to deceive readers as to the narrator's intentions in undertaking the writing of his lifestory. The operations of Guzmán the narrator that I have termed "prudent jester" and "impudent joker" are complementary throughout the development of the novel, not only in the work's plot, but more importantly in the narration whose aims it serves. Joly's impressive study of lexical features in individual narrative *burlas* of the *Guzmán* calls for a comprehensive look at the way that *burlas* structure the entire enunciation of the *pícaro*'s account, through the relation of both temporal levels. Rodríguez's analysis of the narrator's deceptions in the present as author complements the work of the French critic, but his study, similarly, addresses primarily one temporal plane of the narrator's personal history.

The purpose of my own study of Alemán's work, which was begun independently of those of Joly and Rodríguez, has been to analyze the discursive functions, cited above, through which the narrator organizes his alleged autobiography, and then to examine movements within both temporal planes of the literary account of his life that constitute extended *burlas*. Although my conclusions deal with the social judgments that they imply, my primary interest in undertaking the present study of the *Guzmán* was to consider the relationship between the linguistic construction of its *burlas* and the autobiography that they structure. Years of work with Alemán's book have convinced me that the preponderance of this material in both the narrated past and narrating present—from incorporated popular anecdotes, sayings, and witticisms to the narrator's own implicitly learned, rhetoricized verbal distortions of his relationship with society—is intended to serve an exemplary function that goes beyond that of risible negative *exempla*. Sieber's study of the *Lazarillo* (*Language and Society*, x) argues that the anonymous "life" chronicles a process of personal initiation and development that is specifically linguistic in nature: "The nature of his [Lázaro's] 'life' is not a reflection or a representation of an individualized sixteenth-century experience. Rather it is the 'life' of the individualizing acts of language through which such an experience takes form." The narrator's story thereby serves the dual function of educating readers as to the role of language in structuring the terms of their social existence, and provides the keys by which to read its own duplicitous communication. As the following chapters will demonstrate, the *Guzmán*—despite its length and digressions—also unfolds through the narrative of formative experiences in the social use of language and, upon the narrator's initiation, into a system of verbal relationships that results in the composition of his autobiography. The transgressive nature of the boy "Guzmanillo"'s language clearly constitutes an example that readers must not emulate. But in addition, the representation of relationships in language within the narrative illustrates the *burlas* of misleading rhetoric and logic that inform the complex enunciation of the autobiography itself. Guzmán's description of his formation thereby serves as a blueprint for the reading of the literary account dedicated to that very task. To understand the discursive status of the *pícaro*'s autobiography, we must, then, consider the problem of *burlas* and their composition in both temporal levels of Alemán's work, as well as the displacement of operations from one to the other.

The first chapter of this study will examine the constitution of Alemán's narrator Guzmán as a *figura* (figure)—both an identifiable social entity and a figural creation—within the space of his lifestory. In contrast with Reed's excellent study of the novel from the perspective of its implied readers (*Reader in the Picaresque*), my own emphasis will be on the creative process through which the narrator's manipulation of his status vis-à-vis the destinaries of his account forces the reevaluation, in turn, of their positions within the world narrated. By tracing closely the development of Guzmán's narrating voice, I intend to demonstrate that considerations of its sincerity or insincerity do not address the problem actually explored by the use of the first person—that of the multiple, often conflicting terms through which a "self" may be composed. The "I" of Guzmán's account, a pronominal category with the unique status, in Benveniste's terms, of a "shifter," has no reality for readers except in the context created by the narrator's words. Its very lack of extraliterary referentiality, however, enables the fictive autobiographer to select the terms that will compose for readers his social being—his status in their world as "he."[11] At the same time, Guzmán's first-person voice establishes an intersubjective context of communication with them, whose exemplarity is to be found precisely in its discursive mobility: his personal history—a carefully composed view of the narrator's evolving self—is not the medium but the substance itself of his persona. As Friedman argues ("Picaresque as Autobiography," 120), "not only is the teller in the tale, but he is the tale; the narrative act becomes both form and substance of message production."

The second chapter will look at the way in which the temporal plane of the narrator's "history"—or, more appropriately, "story"—represents his dual function as a *figura*. Within my own study, I have referred to this level of articulation, which may also be designated by Benveniste's term *histoire*, generally as the "narrative" and, when considering its integral components in given contexts, as "history" or "story." The narrative of Guzmán's past both sketches the parameters of his highly mobile social identity as a presumptuous trickster, and reveals, through analogic illustrations of his authorial drive to invent guises, the figural status of the final, contemporaneous narration that creates him. This chapter examines three phases in the formative career of the narrator as a prudent jester and an impudent joker: 1) his early victimization by other jokers; 2) the development and refinement, in an oscillating pattern of dependency relationships and independent self-definition, of the narrator's dual discursive functions as trickster; and 3) the circumstances that lead to and include the mature *pícaro*'s bid for authority in exercising the same dual discursive functions, as author of his life. The narrative history of the protagonist Guzmán is at once the exemplary story, or representation, of the misleading, heteroglossic first-person discourse that narrates Guzmán's being in the present and, at the same time, the active problematization within a context of interpersonal dialogue of its dangers for the reader.[12]

The third chapter shifts focus, to consider the process of Guzmán's enunciation of his lifestory as it is organized from the perspective of his authorial present tense. In it, I refer to this plane of articulation—Benveniste's *discours*—as "narration," when focusing upon the weaving of Guzmán's story itself, and "discourse," when referring to problems of voice and perspective in so doing. The purpose of this final segment of my book is not to demonstrate inconsistencies in perspective—paradoxical argumentation or the rhetoric of irony, for example—that might be considered *burlas*, within the other temporal plane of Alemán's work, in and of itself. Other critics, such as Arias (*Unrepentant Narrator*), have already shed considerable light on the complex self-contradictions that characterize the *Guzmán*'s moralizing discourse. Rather, my intention has been to demonstrate the functionally analogic relationship that exists between the work's temporal levels by studying their juncture in specific examples within Guzmán's account. I have selected three episodes of particular prominence within that account—the *pícaro*'s major swindles—because they are the clearest paradigms of the process, in the larger operations that compose the autobiography, through which discursive *burlas* of the narrational present are displaced onto the past. In each case, a narrative context both duplicates and dismantles, within a represented social exchange, the linguistic ambiguity of Guzmán's authorial discourse, showing its potential effects upon society. Yet the exemplarity of the narrated exchange is, at the same time, countered by Guzmán's own authorial misassessments of it, in passages of discourse that bracket and/or bisect the narrative example. The insistence of this diegetic intrusion into the work's narrative episodes, even in those with little ostensible commentary, leads me to argue that the narrative we read does not simply contain *burlas* that are to be discounted as bad examples, or that prefigure the tone of the narrator's mature voice. It develops through the metonymy of the *pícaro*'s verbal function, in represented cases of self-substantiation, the metaphorizing drive of the very work that seeks to define him. In other words, the operations of Guzmán's discourse are displaced onto and repeated in the autobiography's second temporal level to effect its exemplarity, as a positive and entertaining didactic move.

To conclude, my intention in studying Alemán's *pícaro*'s autobiography has been twofold: first, and primarily, to explore the rhetorical, linguistic design linking both narration and narrative in the *Guzmán*, which is exemplary precisely for its attempted challenging of authority; and second, thereby to establish preliminary steps for further study of the incorporation of autobiographic fictions, and the corresponding treatment of invention and authority, in the Spanish picaresque genre.

As a final note of clarification, I have used Brancaforte's edition for all citations of the *Guzmán*. Chapter 3 contains a parenthetical reference to Rico's edition, in my discussion of one quote from the swindle of the Milanese merchant, because Rico's text clarifies a pronominal relationship important to the dialogue under consideration.

1
The "figure" Guzmán

In the centuries since its publication, Mateo Alemán's *Guzmán de Alfarache* has experienced swings of fortune that rival those of its protagonist. Initially a best-seller,[1] whose influence resounded in the pages of Cervantes and in fictive autobiographies that came to constitute the Spanish picaresque, the *Guzmán* was quickly translated abroad.[2] It gave rise to adaptations and parodies on the Continent and in England, which enjoyed immense popularity with the reading public well into the eighteenth century.[3] The nineteenth century, however, saw little interest in the *Guzmán*, and Alemán's novel endured relative neglect until the beginning of the twentieth, when broader interest in social history and the picaresque caused a resurgence in scholarly, if not popular, attention to the Spanish genre. The first modern studies of the *Guzmán*, dedicated largely to tracing the relationship between Alemán's biography and his novel, were complemented in literary histories and studies of the picaresque, such as Chandler's *The Literature of Roguery* (1907), by discussion of possible parallels between the fictive *pícaro* figure and real social deviants.[4] Beginning in the forties, however, *Guzmán* criticism underwent a shift of perspective, as readers began to analyze the ethical and religious themes of its narrator's discourse. One group, the "Catholic-apologetic school," has since described the *Guzmán* as a Counter-reformation monolith, structured by its narrator upon univocal argumentation in the recounting of his wrongs and repentance.[5] Its opponents, meanwhile, find in the same figure's discourse a dualism that conveys a *converso*'s (convert's) ambivalence to the doctrine that he must voice.[6] And to complicate our picture of Guzmán de Alfarache's story, sociocritical studies of the last two decades have found in the novel not the moral struggle of a realistic subject, but the complex articulation through its *pícaro* narrator of conflicting discourses from seventeenth-century Spanish society.[7] As Johnson argues (*Inside Guzmán*, 7–9), Alemán's novel invites many different readings, for the experiences and reflections of its protagonist have both universal and historical resonances.

Clearly, reception of the *Guzmán* has from the outset been closely related to the ways in which its narrating subject is perceived. Different periods and schools of thought have given us a character whose guises—from hardened criminal to moral philosopher—are hard to reconcile, and whose message is equally ambiguous. Smith (*Writing in the Margin*, 79) suggests that our search for a cohesive, modern depiction of subjective experience in the narrator Guzmán does not take into account models and principles of the period during which Alemán wrote. In addition to being anachronistic, he argues (80–81), search for a unifying "point of view" may well reveal our own ideological biases. Sobejano ("El pícaro hablador," 471–74) observes that Guzmán's consistency, in fact, is to be found not in what he says, but simply in the fact that he is an inveterate talker who comments upon himself and all he views. Modern criticism has sought to determine Guzmán's role in the novel in terms that are sociological or psychological, without much discussion of this prominent function of the narrator, perhaps because it is self-evident. Sobejano's argument bears careful consideration, however, for Guzmán's most highly developed function in the work is precisely that of an *hablador*. While his status and motives as a religious convert, moral philosopher, or political adviser are ambiguous, Guzmán's voice is ever present. He is a tireless gossip, a fast-talker, and a long-winded mouthpiece of righteousness. Guzmán establishes his persona by interpreting his behavior and its value linguistically, and the character that we judge, with its nagging inconsistencies, is quite self-consciously composed in his autobiographical account. Moreover, what Guzmán tells us is that he has spent his life as a *pícaro* plying other audiences, characters in the narrative, with fictions of himself.

In the lifestory of Alemán's ambitious narrator, operations implicit in the composition of autobiography, such as selection, figural temporal displacement, and linguistic invention, become the focus of explicit reflection, for Guzmán's narrative studies the ways that he has used them to position and reposition himself in society. The account of his life clearly warns through its examples that self-representation always obeys a purpose and presents an interested view of its subject. Even when elements of truth—at times virtually complete admission of his circumstances—structure Guzmán's presentation of his life to others within the narrative, the truth itself is used in context to deceive—*engañar con la verdad*. In his recent book, *The Changing Nature of Self*, Elbaz takes issue with dominant theories of first-person expression as rhetoricized medium, arguing (8–9) that any linguistic utterance implies organization from the particular perspective of the speaker or writer: "history, science, or for that matter any meaningful statement, in no way duplicate reality, they construct it. For language is functional to the ideological position of the speaking subject, and 'reality' is the creation of this same subject. One does not report, duplicate or verify the truth: one makes it."[8] Far from reporting the truth of a personal existence not witnessed by readers, the enunciation of Guzmán's exemplary autobiographical account constructs the terms in which he wishes his "I" to be perceived by others.

Renza argues in "Veto of the Imagination" (2) that carefully organized references to the narrator's past in effect constitute an interpretation of the authorial present that binds him to readers: "The autobiographer of necessity knows as well as writes about his past from the limiting perspective of his present self-image—*ce qu'il est devenu*—and thus adopts, wanting to express the "truth" about this past, specific verbal strategies in order to transcend such limitation." Zahareas ("Historical Function of Picaresque Autobiographies," 140–41) argues that "a brief paraphrase of some key picaresque *Lives* reveals, self-referentially, this generic pattern of presenting a remembrance of past offenses in the interest of the offender's present. . . . After all, a *pícaro* can intervene in his deviant past only as the writer of that past deviance." In the case of the *Guzmán*, this strategy points the way to the final chapter of Part II, which describes the circumstances of its composition long before readers arrive at their explicit explanation. Guzmán creates the persona, or "figura," as Barros's Eulogy to Part I terms it, of his developing self as an inventive talker, to portray the "I" that he no longer is.[9] At the same time, the end of his account reveals the character of the narrator still to be, within the present of his enunciation, the active creator through language of his own existence—a talker whose composition renders him in figural terms.

In the novel, as readers quickly notice, Alemán has Guzmán propose to edify readers, but in the course of his many sermons and reflections, he is not made to articulate one clear message. Critical debate over the moral or social thesis of his contradictory reflections finds no resolution precisely because, as Sobejano argues, the *pícaro*'s lesson is empirical ("De la intención," 289): his "historia poético-pedagógica" ("poetic-pedagogic story") teaches the dangers of deception through the example of his own literary discourse. Although he considers many issues, from the religious to the political, the primary lesson for readers lies not in what he says, but in how he says it. As Guzmán himself warns readers of the contextual nature of meaning in Chapter 1 (I, 1, 1: 107), speaking of values in an economic register, "Mas lo que se entiende cambio es obra indiferente, de que se puede usar bien y mal" [However, what is meant by exchange is an undifferentiated work, which may be put to good and bad ends]. Signs of religiosity, another, more immediately relevant example, are as subject to redefinition by context as are other signifiers:

> Decir, si veo que un religioso entra a la media noche por una ventana en parte sospechosa, la espada en la mano y el broquel en el cinto, que va a dar los sacramentos, es locura, que ni quiere Dios ni su Iglesia permite que yo sea tonto y de lo tal, evidentemente malo, sienta bien. (107)

> [To say, if I see that an ecclesiastic is entering at midnight by a window in some suspicious place, sword in hand and shield in his belt, that he is going to administer the sacraments, is madness, for neither God nor His Church are going to allow that I be so foolish as to take such behavior, evidently evil, for good.]

While the moralizing content of Guzmán's discourses and sermons has didactic merit, in the context of explaining his own case, as critics argue, even moralizing has the potential for signifying something altogether different. What he says might lack authority and make it impossible for readers to assign to Guzmán one discursive register or one clearly discernible identity. The fact that his words consistently function this way, however, provides readers with an identity in and of itself: Guzmán is a figure who lives by his mouth, an author composed of the rhetorical "figures" of his narration. (To avoid confusion of references to the real author Alemán and to Guzmán as a fictive author, in this study I will hereafter refer to Guzmán's linguistic role simply as that of "narrator." Reed [*Reader in the Picaresque*, 16] makes a good case for referring to Guzmán as "author-in-the-text," but I find the designation cumbersome.)

The narrator seems to establish within the account of his person an implied dialogue or "diálogo hacia,"[10] which appears intended to clarify his message by invoking the scrutiny and criticisms of imagined destinaries. Yet this narrative procedure—bounded by Guzmán's monologue—results in both the suppression of other voices and in greater confusion for readers than may arise from Cervantine dialogue, for he is free to shift perspective and counter his own logic with unchecked liberty in order to share his culpability with readers and thereby diminish his exemplary distinction as a master of deception.[11] The pluralism of Guzmán's discourse, as it echoes the values of varied readers to whom he directs it, has at the same time the important structural function of casting him as a hybrid subject: language enables him to be at once their superior, inferior, and author of the difference, in a society that prefers to draw lines delimiting status along material markers. We must consider that the narrator Guzmán, with a perspicacity that exceeds insights of his implied judges—who seem intent on punishing only material deception such as theft—has identified the real source of lasting power in a society troubled with economic and political instability. His writing, while accomplishing an edifying expiation and self-castigation, will at the same time trick the expectations of readers by immortalizing him as a popular hero, who defines himself with robust disregard for the constraints of his society. After formerly having stripped influential recipients of his communications—from merchants to courtiers—of material indicators of importance, as a thief and confidence man, we find him now translating the terms of their physical existence into verbal relationships of his own composition. In effect, Guzmán responds to those presuming to judge him by becoming the author of their ridicule, as well as his own. Through the narrator's composition of himself and his society, the autobiography we read thus examines both the power of self-writing and the posture of *burla* that informs its deception.

It is not surprising that Guzmán's witty shifts of perspective have resulted in considerable difference of opinion regarding the message of his account. Alemán, however, did not intend for readers to undertake their labors without preparation for the interpretive activity entailed. The Dedication and Prologues, the "Declaración para el entendimiento deste libro" (Statement for the comprehension of this book) and Barros's "Elogio" (Eulogy) inform us of how the narrator communicates and the way his words are intended to characterize him as the novel's subject. These introductory pages have not received much discussion by modern critics. Yet, as Smith notes (*Writing in the Margin*, 99), "the *Guzmán* is concerned explicitly, if intermittently, with the process of representation itself"; segments of the text devoted to theoretical or critical discussion of its subject's self-representation were intended by Alemán to capture his readers' attention. I will add that it is quite deliberately in these preliminary passages that the Tridentine intentions of Alemán's work find their truest articulation, for the narrator whom he has created to compose the following *vida* will teach by *engaño* (deception).

Before proceeding in Section 2 of this chapter to terms of the narrator's own self-definition in the text of his account, Section 1 will first examine definitions of Guzmán as narrator given by Alemán and Barros in the pages that open the novel. As Reed has pointed out (*Reader in the Picaresque*, 16), the oscillating psychological postures of Guzmán himself, with respect to his work's real and implied destinaries, make our assessment of the reading demanded by his account extremely difficult. It is therefore important that we attempt to localize within Alemán's work references to the context from which the narrator's act of writing emerges. This system of allusions begins in the segments that introduce the work, and it is elaborated within a semantic field that requires careful examination. I apologize to my own readers for what may appear to be unnecessary digression into preliminary materials. While the Dedication, Prologues, and the "Entendimiento" follow standard rhetorical formulae, their lexical composition is centered on terms highly charged with irony from the Prologue and Tratados of the *Lazarillo*—"algo" (something), "bueno" (good), "aprovechar" (to take advantage). Through their use, Alemán in effect prefigures the discourse through which the narrating *pícaro* will relate his autobiography, thereby alerting readers to the multi-level reading the text will demand of them. The didactic aims of Alemán's introduction, in fact, are better accomplished by displaced allusions to the dangers of his narrator's voice—that is, by Alemán himself modeling the discursive voice of his character—than by clear explanation of the latter's present circumstances. Accompanying this presentation of Guzmán are two Prologues intended to relieve Alemán of responsibility for the work's reception—negative or positive. Alemán's invocations of *discretos lectores* (prudent readers) and the *vulgo* (the general public) allude to their different levels of intellectual acumen; nevertheless, he assigns to them functional definitions that are distinctly social, depending upon their response to his work: in effect, we find, all critics pertain to the *vulgo* while those who favor its composition, whether they understand it or not, are *discretos lectores*. The "Entendimiento" that closes Alemán's opening situates his narrator, problematically, on the gallows steps. Finally, Barros's Euology warns that Guzmán is a "figura," using a term whose multiple definitions signal the relationship to follow, in the story of Guzmán's life, between art and society.

Through analysis, first of Alemán's introductory materials (in Section 1, "The 'inconstant figure of this discourse'"), and second, of the narrator's own statement of his literary function within the narrative that follows (in Section 2, "'An accepted courtier'"), I will undertake to show that the *Guzmán de Alfarache* is, self-consciously, a study in the power of writing to fashion and position its subject, while questioning relationships in language that structure his society. If Alemán's *pícaro* is to be the object of self-writing that will censure his behavior as it immortalizes him, so too must readers—his judges—become objects of the same literary "record." The *pícaro* Guzmán will submit to sentencing by prudent readers, but, ironically, he insists upon speaking for them, with their language as well as his. The terms of both Alemán and his account suggest that as poet the narrator expresses simultaneously the views of a joker or social deviant and those of a toadying court jester, as he redraws with wit the lines of discursive power that should guarantee the authority of readers to judge him.

The "inconstant figure of this discourse"

As he commends the novel to readers, Alemán, in a brief but prominent series of statements, warns of his narrator's criminality and capacity for devious behavior as author. We learn in the closing words of the Dedication to the Marquis of Poza that the novel's subject is a "pícaro," who has been given the aspiration of entering court circles:

> Conseguiráse juntamente que, haciendo mucho lo que de suyo es poco, de un desechado pícaro un admitido cortesano, será dar ser a lo que no lo tiene.... (I: 81)
>
> [It will also happen that, making greater what is little his, of a rejected rogue an accepted courtier, will be to give being to that which has none....]

And in the paragraph devoted to describing Guzmán in the "Declaración," Alemán clarifies that this *pícaro* has drawn on experience as a trickster, man of letters, and man of the cloth to compose during his free time as a galley slave the account that we read (I: 88–89). It functions, he adds, similarly to less eloquent "sermoncitos" (short sermons) routinely delivered by convicts on the gallows steps:

> Y no es impropriedad ni fuera de propósito si en esta primera [parte] escribiere alguna dotrina; que antes parece muy llegado a razón darla un hombre de claro entendimiento, ayudado de letras y castigado del tiempo, aprovechándose del ocioso de la galera. Pues aun vemos a muchos

ignorantes justiciados, que habiendo de ocuparlo en sola su salvación, divertirse della por estudiar un sermoncito para en la escalera. (I: 89)

[And it is no impropriety, nor unsuitable, if in this first (part) he writes some doctrine; rather, it seems quite reasonable that a man of sharp mind deliver it, aided by letters and punished by time, while taking advantage of the idle (time) of the galley. For we even see many ignorant criminals who, having to occupy it (their time) solely to the end of their salvation, distract themselves for fun by studying a little sermon for (delivery) on the steps.]

Sobejano observes ("De la intención," 289) that the *pícaro*'s repentance and conversion were clearly superimposed in Part II upon Alemán's original didactic thesis for the novel in order to motivate the end of Guzmán's adventures as a rogue and thus the end to spurious continuations of his exploits. At the beginning of Part I, Alemán, in fact, entrusts to readers the self-explanation of a "castigado" (punished man), which has been produced by the very "ocio" (idle time) responsible for his previous crimes.[12] Readers receive clear warning, thus, that the narrator of the autobiography they read is a well-educated social deviant who seeks to win the favor of highly placed readers while he is precariously close to the gallows. A "buen estudiante, latino, retórico y griego" (good student, Latin scholar, rhetorician, and master of Greek) who then studied religion (I: 88–89), he has availed himself of the discourses of his readers and "idle time of the galley" to do, we must presume, what he has done with time on his hands before—deceive.

Alemán's explicit statements in his introductory passages regarding his narrator's linguistic abilities seem intended to guarantee guidelines for reading the *Guzmán* that the elliptical, enigmatic Prologue to the *Lazarillo*, voiced by the *pícaro* himself, omits. Indeed this extra presence strikes readers initially as a safeguard against the dangers of the protagonist's self-introduction. However, Alemán withholds information about the social identity that Guzmán's narrative aims to chronicle and perhaps to improve, and he does not explain the crimes that led to it. Alemán's references to the narrator of this edifying novel do little more than whet our curiosity about the specifics of the latter's life and alert us to the discursive complexity with which Guzmán's account may be composed. The explicit focal point of Alemán's didactic intentions in these opening pages, then, is the language of his character's autobiography. The reader's attention is directed at the same time, but only by veiled allusion, to a second and equally important concern: the power of that language to forge complex social relationships. Yet while readers are prepared for the figural complexity of Guzmán's writing both by explicit mention of his training and by Alemán's use of the same language in his introductory lines, information about potential social effects of the *pícaro*'s communication upon its recipients is withheld.

The readers of Alemán's introductory segments must surely have recalled the curious lack of detail regarding the personal case of another narrator requested to explain his relationship with a superior and his community, in the Prologue to the *Lazarillo*. Although we can only guess at the degree to which Alemán sought consciously to produce this effect, the basic analogy between the quasi-judicial contexts from which both protagonists relate their "lives" in order to be judged and the evasive rhetoric with which they do so would certainly have alerted Alemán's contemporaries—readers of the 1573 *Lazarillo castigado*, if not copies of the original text—to resonances of the latter's Prologue in the Introduction to the *Guzmán*. In order to prepare readers for his narrator without divulging the latter's secrets, Alemán brilliantly reinforces his brief references to Guzmán's linguistic training by writing in the manner that the latter will communicate. In the process, he parodies the rhetoric and semantic registers of the *Lazarillo*. Both traces of the sixteenth-century novel and Alemán's method, in anticipating the voice of Guzmán, become more evident in each successive introductory section.

To begin with, in his Dedication of the novel in Part I to the Marquis of Poza, "don Francisco de Rojas," Alemán devotes three of four paragraphs to the promotion of himself and his literary talent, with the usual rhetorical commonplaces. We glean the first information about the narrator only in the final lines of the Dedication, and Alemán does not explain his reference. With provocative irony, he requests that his patron make "of a rejected rogue an accepted courtier" (I: 81). Whether the narrator himself will be made to entertain such pretensions within the plot of the novel or in his narrative discourse is left to our judgment in the perusal of pages to follow. While Alemán declines to discuss the reference, however, the allusions that follow strongly suggest an analogy between Alemán's aims for his book and those that will be attributed to the book's subject.[13] Alemán's own reference to the protagonist of Part I in authorizing a 1602 reprinting reinforces this analogy: "Sepan ... que por cuanto yo tengo licencia del Rey nuestro señor para poder ynprimir en sus rreynos un libro yntitulado guzmán del alfarache, que por otro nombre se llama el pícaro cortesano ... [Let it be known ... that for as long as I have permission of the King our Lord to be able to print in his kingdoms a book entitled 'guzmán de alfarache,' that by another name is called 'The courtly *pícaro*' . . .].[14]

Alemán begins by conflating attributes of his own voice with those of the narrator Guzmán, thereby alerting observant readers to the wit that will structure the narrative discourse of the latter. As the arrogant offerer of a "don tan pobre" (such a poor gift), the novel we hold, Alemán, as well as the narrator behind whom he stands, will certainly suffer the prejudicial criticisms of readers with "mala intención" (evil intention) and "bajos pensamientos" (base thoughts)—in short, the *vulgo*, or general public (I: 79). Its members are, we read, marked by "lowly blood" and "humble birth," hereditary disadvantages that deny them the noble patron's privileged social rank and cause their envious calumny of others whose quest for acceptance threatens to meet with reward (I: 80–81). The negative reactions anticipated on the part of this general public, to both himself and to the narrator within his text, find expression in Alemán's dual references to his fears for the occasion presented by the potentially successful novel. He admits that he will be slandered as brazen for offering to a nobleman and courtier such a subject: "calumniándo*me*, cuando menos, de temerario atrevido, pues a tan poderoso principe haya tenido ánimo de ofrecer un don tan pobre . . ." [slandering *me*, at the very least, as a foolhardy upstart, since to such a powerful prince I have had the nerve to offer such a poor gift . . .]. And he voices the hope that his book will be protected from libel by the influence of its patron: ". . . seguro estoy del generoso ánimo de V. Señoría que, estendiendo las alas de su acostumbrada clemencia, debajo dellas quedará mi libro libre de los que pudieran calumniar*le*" [I am certain of Your Lordship's generous spirit that, spreading the wings of your accustomed mercy, beneath them my book will remain safe from those who could slander *it*] (I: 80, my emphasis). Alemán thus seeks, by analogy, a common fate for both himself and his creation, when he adds that this favor of his book will in effect make "of a rejected rogue an accepted courtier" (I: 81).

Although the real author's bourgeois background and his narrator's truly marginal, lower-class status would seem to consign both to the ranks of the *vulgo*, or general public (that is, those marked by "lowly blood" and "humble birth"), Alemán—a writer for money and not a member of court literary circles—boldly demands the rewards that his narrating *pícaro* is made to pursue: acceptance through favor into the courtly ranks that blood and economic hardship have denied him. This posture on the part of Alemán makes perfect sense when the vicissitudes of his personal history are considered.[15] Equally important for comprehension of his novel, the words "of a rejected rogue an accepted courtier" at the same time provide clues to the motives underlying that deceptive voice of Guzmán through which Alemán speaks. The real author's creation, his book, risks slander because it is the self-heralding literary account not of his own existence but that of a *pícaro* who has been rejected by society—in figurative terms by virtue of his birth and, "literally," within the story of his life, to serve time as a convicted criminal. The daring of Alemán lies clearly in the daring of the narrating subject that he has created: Guzmán the *pícaro* is made to seek preferential treatment from his judges, paradoxically, both in spite of and in return for his narrated crimes. The framing provided by Alemán's dedication of the novel thus anticipates the narrator Guzmán's own dedication of his account, at its end (in II, 3, 9), to those superiors—and to one in particular—who, similarly "spreading the wings of his accustomed mercy" (I: 80), may make him, although a galley slave, an "accepted courtier," as the favorite author of courtiers. Thus, with the double referentiality of his initial dedication, Alemán expresses his own hopes for the book's positive reception by its patron and by extension by other influential readers. He simultaneously begins to prepare our perceptions of the narrator's intentions. In effect, Guzmán the criminal's book is aimed at establishing first its narrator, and thereby Alemán, as a *discreto* among *discretos*, a figure endowed with both the intellectual and social superiority that privilege the likes of Francisco de Rojas.

By invoking rhetorical commonplaces standard in dedications and prologues—the authorial apology, eulogy of the work's patron, and invective against its potential critics—the opening Dedication of Alemán's work to Francisco de Rojas lays the groundwork for complex references to follow, to the "vulgo" and to a singular "discreto lector." The more prolonged Prologues to each of these audiences in the next pages take Alemán's references to them beyond the vitriolic disclaimers and hyperbolic encomiums traditionally expected in the treatment of this literary topic, however.[16] Critics such as Ife (*Reading and Fiction in Golden-Age Spain*, 128) and Reed (*Reader in the Picaresque*, 14–16) remind us that reader reception of the work has been made, from the outset, an important structural component of the narrator Guzmán's personal account, as well as the concern of Alemán. Those members of the public who may affect the fortunes of the latter and his book and who could implicitly determine the fate of the figure Guzmán take on fuller contours, as they gain the status of potential characters, respondents to what Sobejano ("De Alemán a Cervantes," 729) has argued is the *pícaro*'s implied dialogue.

In his explicit designation of two separate audiences to whom are attributed distinct levels of reading competency, Alemán, Reed reminds us (18), initiated a Golden Age literary convention. The reason for the dual address of five lengthy paragraphs to the *vulgo* and another seven under separate heading to the *discreto lector* appears to have been an intent to clarify the terms of his book's potential reception by the reading public. If we compare the *Guzmán*'s Prologues to the single one of its predecessor, the *Lazarillo*, Alemán appears bent on deconstructing the ambiguities that open the anonymous "life." In framing Part I of the novel by directing two radically different classes of destinaries to divergent readings of its contents, however, he makes it clear that ambiguity will in fact be a fundamental structure in his novel as well. Parodying the fictive Lázaro's dedication of his account to "alguno" (someone) and "muchos" (many) (I: 91), Alemán presents his book to an astute minority deemed to possess the critical awareness necessary for correct interpretation of the message underlying Guzmán's narrative, and to average readers who will enjoy reading the narrator's account at face value, while overlooking the potential referentiality of his figurative allusions.

Critics have demonstrated that in the *Lazarillo*, the invocation of dual audiences is motivated from within the plot by the rhetorical design of the novel.[17] Given the function of this dual reading public in the rhetorical designs that structure the narrative of the *Lazarillo*, we must consider carefully the way in which they are invoked again in the *Guzmán*. They are brought into play precisely in the Prologue, which expresses Alemán's intent to give us the keys to a correct interpretation of Guzmán the convict's autobiography. And yet his dedicatories to these two groups place responsibility for interpretation of the renowned liar's account squarely on their shoulders. His separate Prologues for two classes of readers explicitly highlight problems of interpretation, while denying at the same time answers that might alleviate the difficulties inherent in the hermeneutic activity demanded of readers.[18]

Alemán turns his attention first to the age-old deficiencies of the *vulgo*, with a predictably rhetorical invective. Readers learn both that correct interpretation is their responsibility and that their own shortcomings will impede proper assessment of the communication offered to them. With the adversarial stance to be expected in this dedication, Alemán argues that the *vulgo*'s limited capacity for comprehension is conditioned by self-interest; denial of the merits of others makes it "tardo en honrar" (late to honor) (I: 82). Clearly, the *vulgo* will be of no help to Alemán or his subject in their quest for favor: "Bien cierto estoy que no te ha de corregir la protección que traigo ni lo que a su calificada nobleza debes . . ." [I am quite certain that the protection I bring will not correct you, nor what you owe his attested nobility . . .] (I: 83). Projecting their subjectivity upon the object perceived, members of the general public, we learn, devaluate the latter's attributes to match their own: "¿Qué santidad no calumnias? ¿Qué inocencia no persigues? ¿Qué sencillez no condenas?" [Is there any saintliness that you do not slander? What innocence do you not pursue? What simplicity do you not condemn?] (I: 82).

In effect, those who respond to Guzmán's autobiography negatively, with punishment or other forms of criticism, may find themselves berated as the *vulgo*, whether or not their judgment results from sharp observation of wrongs that merit it. Readers are led to suspect early on, as Reed points out (*Reader in the Picaresque*, 70–72), that the designations "vulgo" and "discretos" are mobile terms. I suggest that the designations are assigned according to the reader's implied power relationship with both Alemán and his creation. Ironically, those readers who exercise power over Alemán and his subject, in unfavorable judgments, are ridiculed as undiscerning—in effect, the *vulgo*; even those motivated to do so by critical insights that should label them "discretos" may well fall into this category, for Alemán through Guzmán will question their perceptions. We must indeed wonder whether—as a corollary—"discretos" might not refer in fact simply to readers who favor the *pícaro*'s autobiography, regardless of its deceptions.

Alemán argues that many readers are swift to attribute to others the faults that they themselves with hypocrisy conceal. In so doing, they may slander the innocent. An indication of the excesses of the general public, even "illustrious men," the leaders of society, are branded with the traits of this offensive subject as "jokers," "incontinents,"[19] and "liars": "atrevidamente has mordido a tan ilustres varones, graduando a los unos de graciosos, a otros acusando de lascivos y a otros infamando de mentirosos" [You have insolently gnawed at illustrious men, appraising some as comics, accusing others of lewdness, and defaming others as liars] (I: 83). In the contiguity of Alemán's clever reasoning, those whom the *vulgo* criticizes as "comics" and "liars"—society's most discountable voices—may in fact be worthy of its greatest respect: "illustrious men." The desire expressed in the closing lines of his previous Dedication that an unreliable *pícaro* be welcomed to the ranks of the social elite as an "accepted courtier" echoes here as a concern that informs the communication to be established with readers. While we learn of the common readers' disparaging misapprehension of their betters, or *discretos*, as "comics," we learn at the same time that "graciosos" in fact may be "illustrious men." Correct identification of this status presumably determines our own rank as readers: to be *discretos*, readers must restore to the alleged "comic" the respect due him. With the cleverness that will pervade Guzmán's voice, Alemán's rhetoric thus prepares readers for upcoming characterizations of his narrator as an astute "comic" who merits their respect for the wise advice that his account conveys. He also hints at the terms of Guzmán's relationship with those who judge him: he will gain entry to the ranks of courtiers by performing as the only inferior whose wit qualifies him to address them directly—a jester whose threat to their importance is concealed by a posture of self-deprecation.

The following Prologue, "Del mismo al discreto lector" (From the same to the prudent reader), further develops the interests of Alemán in marketing his novel, with a predictable modification of tone. Ironically, after Alemán has provided virtually no direct guidelines for interpretation to that reading public deemed most in need of it, here readers find some explanation of his intentions and method. They receive, in fact, wholesale invitation to join the elite company of the *discreto lector*, and find patronizing instructions on how to assure for themselves this desirable status. Reed asserts (*Reader in the Picaresque*, 68) that "the tradition of medieval hermeneutics of deciphering hidden or secret meanings is required by this Baroque text." Alemán states specifically that for fear of giving offense, his figurative language has both "touched up" or altered the appearance of some referents and incompletely sketched others by allusion (I: 86).

The narration of his work is characterized by an arsenal of rhetorical figures and tropes, which are masterfully analyzed by Cros (*Protée et le gueux*) and by Barbara Davis ("The Style of Mateo Alemán's *Guzmán de Alfarache*"). Although the patterns of narrative discourse through which the subject Guzmán himself takes shape are predicated on figural repetition that finds expression in the text as both metaphor and metonymy, as my Chapters 2 and 3 will attempt to demonstrate, much of what he says is articulated through irony. Alemán's Prologue to *discretos* warns readers to consider carefully references that appear to be "barreduras al muladar del olvido" (sweepings to the dungheap of oblivion) for the "escobilla de precio" (valuable gold or silver sweepings) that they conceal (I: 86–87). Not only does Alemán use signifiers that normally denote or connote base referents to convey meaning that will be of value to the readers; in this system of contradictions, much of what he wishes to emphasize is left unstated: "Mucho te digo que deseo decirte, y mucho dejé de escribir que te escribo" [I say much to you that I wish to say, and I refrained from penning much of what I write to you] (I: 86). Silence speaks in the *Guzmán*, and in this introduction Alemán assigns central importance to those references that are suppressed or only partially declared.[20] The focus precisely on ellipses in a text that will characterize itself as aggressively self-reflective and diegetic seems strangely out of keeping with Alemán's avowed didactic intentions, until we remind ourselves that in the narrative to follow he will speak through the voice of "un pícaro el sujeto deste libro" [a rogue, the subject of this book] (I 87). Guzmán's reticence about his life will constitute a heavily loaded register, as did Lázaro's silence regarding the "no sé qué y sí sé qué" [I don't know what and yes I do know what] of his case (Ricapito's edition of the *Lazarillo*, 201).[21]

Alemán's original readers cannot have overlooked the linguistic field in which these references to rhetorical method find discussion. His parody of Pliny's adage, "considerando no haber libro tan malo donde no se halle algo bueno" [considering that there is no book so bad that it contains nothing good] (I: 85), recalls a more immediate echo of the same formula in the *Lazarillo*: "Y a este propósito dice Plinio que no hay libro por malo que sea que no tenga alguna cosa buena" [And for this purpose Pliny says that there is no book so bad that it doesn't contain something good] (91–92). The underlying presence of this predecessor discloses itself with particular force in Alemán's invocation of semantic fields charged in the *Lazarillo* with ironic meaning, beginning with the use of "bueno" (good) and "algo" (something).[22] Alemán's citation of Pliny occurs at the center of a statement of intent that associates "bueno" and "algo" with a third term of key importance in the framing of the *Lazarillo*, "aprovechar" (to profit from) (I: 85).[23]

It is important to recall the context in which the narrator Lázaro sought to "profit from" writing his memoirs. Suggesting first that readers—most specifically "alguno" (someone)—might find "algún fruto" (some benefit) in his otherwise unworthy account (92), Lázaro then clarifies (93) that he himself also hopes to profit, with recompense in the form of fame rather than riches. Shortly thereafter we learn that this recipient, "Vuestra Merced" (Your Grace), is both the narrator's social superior and, more specifically, an authority who possesses the right to demand his testimony and presumably to affect the future of Lázaro's prosperity. The Prologue alone provides insufficient context for our correct reading of Lázaro's use of the adjective "good," with its allusions in the closing words "good port" (97) to the currently successful life that he would presumably like to continue. But Tratado 1 quickly clarifies that "good" is a metaphoric conflation of the expected moral or ethical definition with the economic meaning "well-to-do"—a state, we soon learn, achieved by immoral and illegal behavior. The self-righteous tone of the Prologue gives way to ironic wit, as Lázaro's Tratados reveal his formation in the pursuit of that "buen puerto," or "good life," under the tutelage of his ambitious mother and a series of scurrilous masters after she sells him into service. The narrator Lázaro, having learned well the flexibility of language, the medium that guarantees his survival, in defining the terms of "goodness," himself introduces the narrative to us with the same linguistic mobility that characterizes the variable definitions assigned by "others" to the facts of their material existence, and with the same end: he hopes to get by, preferably with economic comfort and some modicum of social prestige. The narrator Lázaro never refers to himself as a "courtier," but the description of his "new" used clothing in Tratado 6 (198) and of his annexation to the residence of the archpriest of Toledo, who answers to the powerful "Vuestra Merced" (201), obviates the narrator's need of more specific ironic reference. Lázaro's final and current "pinnacle of all good fortune" (205), as the holder of royal office (and several unofficial ones that make him indispensable to those with social honor and power), tells readers that Lázaro considers himself equally deserving of the respect that his associates receive. Without needing to identify his objective, Lázaro presumes, in effect, to the state that Alemán with similar irony will later request for his own *pícaro*, that of an "accepted courtier."

To return to the eruption of Lázaro's language in Alemán's introductory lines, we must consider once again the latter's avowed desire "to profit" (I: 85). There is nothing in Alemán's Prologue to the *discreto lector* or in the "Declaración" that follows to suggest that his own intentions are presented with the irony encoded in Lázaro's discourse. Nor does the information that Alemán gives about himself lead us to suspect self-serving motives beyond his bid for the favor of important readers in the Dedication to Francisco de Rojas. The embedding of "good," "something," and "to profit" in an otherwise neutral discourse, however, signals the intent to mobilize in readers certain semantic associations. Familiar with the fictive Lázaro's rhetorical use of the same signifiers, they will be prepared, without explanatory discourse on the part of Alemán, for the language of the *pícaro* whose case they are to consider. In the middle of verbose clarifications concerning his intentions and method as real author, Alemán again alerts us through the figural nature of his own language to the discursive function of the character who will voice "things . . . sketched" and "touched up," and omit other important references altogether. As "un pícaro el sujeto deste libro" (a rogue, the subject of this book), Guzmán will both charm and impress readers with the wit of his language, and he will work to deceive them. Interestingly enough, nowhere does Alemán state in the dedication to prudent readers that the moralizing discourse voiced by the novel's narrator is true or sincere. Nor does he exhort readers to accept the latter's advice. In fact, he concludes with the reminder that readers will be authors of the moralizing discourse through which the story is to be correctly interpreted, noting that they will find ample text to comment: "En el discurso *podrás* moralizar según se te ofreciere: larga margen te queda" [In the discourse *you* will be able to moralize according to what is presented you] (I: 87, my emphasis). No particular authority is transferred to what Guzmán says; instead, readers are alerted by the echo of the *Lazarillo* in Alemán's language to look for clear indications of the narrator's character and motives, beyond what he says to how he says it.

It becomes clear in the "Declaration for the comprehension of this book" that concludes Alemán's exordiums that Guzmán's most prominent trait is his ability and training at fashioning communication, and through it, himself. Guzmán has become what he is through language. Trained in the first part of the trivium, he traverses the narrative initially as a student and an apprentice in the art of communication. Continuing his formal studies, he extends linguistic mastery to sermonic argumentation, presenting himself as a preacher, as he parodies the authoritative voice of a moralist. And finally, a full complement of natural and learned abilities launches him on a dual linguistic career in which he becomes famous both as a fast-talking criminal and the entertaining narrator of his *historia* (in the senses, we will find, of both "history" and "story"):

> Para lo cual se presupone que Guzmán de Alfarache, nuestro pícaro, habiendo sido muy buen estudiante, latino, retórico y griego, como diremos en esta primera parte, después dando la vuelta de Italia en España, pasó adelante con sus estudios, con ánimo de profesar el estado de la religión; mas por volverse a los vicios los dejó, habiendo cursado algunos años en ellos. El mismo escribe su vida desde las galeras, donde

queda forzado al remo, por delitos que cometió, habiendo sido ladrón famosísimo, como largamente lo verás en la segunda parte. (I: 89)

[For which purpose (to allay the readers' doubts concerning the verisimilitude of Guzmán's account) one must presuppose that Guzmán de Alfarache, our rogue, having been a very fine student, Latin scholar, rhetorician, and master of Greek, as we will explain in this first part, after returning from Italy to Spain, continued further with his studies, with the desire to profess a religious state; but to return to his vices he left off with his studies, having spent several years assiduously at them. He himself writes his life from the galleys, where he is condemned to rowing for crimes he committed, having been an infamous thief, as you will see at length in the second part.]

Alemán motivates the presentation of his character as a lifelike subject through the verisimilar chronology of Guzmán's stages of learning and development, much as we have seen previously in the *Lazarillo*. And yet his focus remains fixed quite particularly on steps in Guzmán's linguistic education rather than on periods of his social or physical development. It is through the narrative of this training that readers will be alerted to the effects of the *pícaro*'s language upon his society, thereby learning the primary lesson that his carefully composed "history" conveys: the ascending complexity of his discursive stages is paired in the novel with our narrator's descending morality; at the summit of his oratorical and literary prowess at the novel's end, Guzmán writes simultaneously from the moral nadir of his criminality. The linguistic virtuosity that will bring the narrator the admiration of highly placed readers is precisely what earlier enabled him to subvert the authority of similar recipients of his communications.

The chronological structure that motivates the narrator's existence in this "Declaration" accompanies the highlighting again of Guzmán's verbal abilities through Alemán's language. Alemán leads into a final reference to his narrator indirectly by alluding first to the behavior that might be expected of a criminal in less control of his powers: even ignorant convicts will devote their free time while serving sentence to attempts to save themselves: "Pues *aun* vemos a muchos *ignorantes justiciados*, que habiendo de ocuparlo [el tiempo "ocioso de la galera"] en sola su salvación, divertirse della por estudiar un sermoncito para en la escalera" [Since we *even* see many *ignorant convicts*, who having to occupy the idle time of the galley solely with the pursuit of their salvation, distract themselves by studying a little sermon for delivery on the steps] (I: 89, my emphasis). The "even" and "ignorant" of Alemán's reference provide the initial terms of a comparison that readers are compelled to supply: how much more so, then, will criminals who are in full command of their actions pursue the same ends. By demanding that readers complete the logical sequence and that they ponder the ambiguity of the term "salvation," this allusion mobilizes our active critical participation in reading, as have other examples of Alemán's indirection. To qualify as *discretos*, readers must examine signifiers that are "merely sketched" or "touched up" for the meaning they may conceal, and supply the suppressed terms of his arguments. Yet they receive no clear directions for assigning values to the ambiguous references of which Alemán warns.

In explanation of the volumes in which his work will be published, aimed at publicizing his rights to the entire project, Alemán concludes the paragraph devoted to defining the motivation of his protagonist with the most concise and yet most loaded description of him so far. As Longhurst insists in his astute refutation of recent theories of Guzmán's conversion ("Conversion and Repentance"), readers must closely examine Alemán's selection not only of the autobiographical narrative but also of the circumstances that motivate his narrator's account. Present-tense references within the work to Guzmán's composition of his lifestory while in chains from early in Part I, the critic asserts (102–4), suggest instead the narrator's desire to regain the approval of society by telling his life. He adds (106): "in creating a literary persona for himself Guzmán seeks to achieve the success and popularity that he has always craved. The end of his account coincides, significantly, with the royal pardon and the end of his imprisonment." While Longhurst joins critics who believe that the narrative ends with Guzmán's freedom to continue his tale in the world beyond the galley, I suggest instead, as subsequent sections will argue, that the approval sought is both figural—fame—and implicitly material—the granting of a commutation that he himself refers to in his closing line with the future subjunctive ("si el cielo me la diere" [if heaven might see fit to grant it to me] [II: 480]). This surprise is reserved for the final page of the autobiography, however. Readers learn in Alemán's introductory pages only that for unexplained reasons Guzmán pens, in the form of the book we read, an account of his life that may function as a "a brief sermon for delivery on the steps."

The ironic disjunction between the projected length of the multi-volume autobiography and the linguistic misnomer "sermoncito" (brief sermon) recalls the verbal economy of Lázaro's deceptions, and arouses readers' suspicions of similar wit in the depiction of subjectivity that will flow from Guzmán's pen. Although specifics of Guzmán's own case remain unclarified at this point, the potential complex of meanings bound by the noun "sermoncito" models for us how the narrator is to communicate, and it hints at possible didactic intentions of his account: the irony of the language with which he deconstructs his "previous" communications will: 1) exhort readers to consider their own behavior by comparing and contrasting it with his example, 2) form his religious confession, and 3) comprise a judicial deposition that may affect his temporal fate as he awaits the gallows. Through the very lack of explanatory circumlocution surrounding it, this brief figurative bait draws readers' attention to one of Alemán's clearest admonitions: Guzmán may speak on his own behalf as well as to help others, and his didactic narration may well conflate multiple discourses in a manner that will make it impossible for them to reduce his message to univocity.

The narrator Guzmán's primary motive for composing the nine-hundred page "little sermon" we read, however, will be his own salvation, in echo of the case that Lázaro so carefully composed on his own behalf. The aggressive verbosity of the "sermonette" dedicated to this purpose should serve perhaps as notice not of the narrator's desire for our welfare so much as his desire that his diegetic edification of readers on the matter of his life cover every angle, obviating the necessity of additional and possibly contradictory testimony by others. As in the case of Lázaro, the narrator Guzmán employs his linguistic mastery to represent through his own voice the voices of others, and in so doing he silences interpretations of his life that are beyond the control of his own narration in the larger world of communication that constitutes society. In composing a literary account of himself, he simply rewrites the dialogic context that has constrained him before, by disguising an extended monologue as implied dialogue. And in parodying the language of his judges, Guzmán simultaneously redefines the target of his critical harangue. The renowned hypocrite and liar cannot criticize himself without ridiculing those whose judgments he mimics, for the polysemia of his language undermines the authority of their discourses.

The fact that the narrator Guzmán is defined by the language with which he composes his life is nowhere more evident than in Barros's "Eulogy" to Part I. In this final admonitory introduction, Guzmán is designated as a "figura" (figure). Cautioning readers to determine carefully their fate as either members of the general public or as prudent readers, Barros advises them to conduct their lives as the "antípoda de la figura inconstante deste discurso" [antipode of the inconstant figure of this discourse] (I: 91). The figure of the discourse to follow is unreliable precisely because his self-representation is figural.[24] As examples of his narration to be discussed in Chapters 2 and 3 clearly reveal, the subject Guzmán is no more than the product of careful composition—in Greenblatt's terms, narrative "self-fashioning"—with language that explores its full potential for multiple referentiality.[25] Guzmán's self-representation with language is furthermore, as another contemporary definition of the term *figura* drives home, a clear indicator of his pretensions to social ascent. The jocose register of *figura*'s secondary meaning in fact reinforces Alemán's hints that his narrator functions as a joker who seeks the favor of courtiers. The seventeenth-century *Diccionario de autoridades* defines the word *figura* (s.v.) metaphorically as "a jocose term for an arrogant man who puts on airs, trying to impress others by communicating with feigned seriousness or gravity" ("[figura] se llama jocosamente al hombre entonado, que afecta gravedad en sus acciones y palabras"). By extension, such a subject should be identified as an "hombre ridículo, feo y de mala traza" [a ridiculous man, improper and with harmful designs].[26] The "inconstant figure of this discourse," Guzmán, adopts the posture of a moralizing preacher, apparently with deceptive intentions, or "mala traza," as a literary joker. His words, as Alemán has already warned, are not to be taken at face value.

Although Alemán refuses to state directly that Guzmán is not just a liar but a criminal, instead preferring to alert us to the narrator's social status only by allusion, Barros decides to add further explanation. Building on Alemán's pointed reference to Guzmán's "brief sermon for delivery on the steps," Barros adds that the character is a "product of idleness" who did not find favor, but instead "pagó con un vergonzoso fin las penas de sus culpas" [paid with a shameful end the penalties for his faults], wearing the "librea" (livery) (I: 90–91) of a galley slave. Despite this clarification, Barros fears that readers will attribute to Alemán the devious motives that direct his narrator's writing: "Y si esto no le salvare de la rigurosa censura e inevitable contradición de la diversidad de pareceres, no será de espantar . . ." [And if this does not save him from severe condemnation and inevitable contradiction of the diversity of views, it will come as no surprise . . .] (I: 93). Although Alemán flatters the presumptions of prestigious readers in two of his introductory sections, according to Barros, readers will clearly define themselves as either members of the general public or prudent readers, not on the basis of their birth and socio-economic standing but through their ability, or lack thereof, to engage in active deciphering of the "inconstant figure of this discourse," or Guzmán's shifting self-portrayal in a discourse of unstable signifiers. It is crucial that they exercise sharp judgment, however, for while Alemán depicts this figure for didactic ends, the subject of the novel himself uses the representation of language to deceive.

The introduction to Alemán's novel thus leaves readers with few specific details regarding the narrator's life or crimes, and plenty of doubts about their own critical faculties. The noticeable absence in Part II of reference, in separate Prologues, to two classes of readers attests to the *discretos*' loss of privileged status as the novel progresses. We must assume that readers initially favored by Alemán's flattery, having also subsidized Martí's Second Part, are ultimately consigned to the company of the common reader, or *vulgo*. Brancaforte (*¿Conversión o proceso de degradación?*, 147) observes that the notable lack of separate Prologues in Part II would seem to reinforce the impression that the same characteristics are ultimately attributed to all readers. Thus Alemán's and Barros's use of the figures, allusions, and ellipses through which Guzmán is made to articulate his discourse aim in Part I to prepare "prudent readers" for an active reading of the novel to follow. But as the novel progresses, the capabilities of both classes of reader are represented with doubt.

"An accepted courtier"

Guzmán the narrator redoubles Alemán's efforts to instruct us about his method in the Dedications by constantly drawing our attention to the medium of his narration from the novel's opening pages forward. He frames the novel with a beginning that provides a model for his narrative procedure in the rest of the book. Although Guzmán states his intention on the first page to explain his life or the "difinido" (that defined) of his account, according to the norm or "difinición" by which it should be measured, he undermines the standards that are to provide a context for our interpretation, and the discourse by which his society formulates them. With oratorical flourishes and step-by-step logic resonant with legalese, Guzmán vows to open the account of his life with a description of his antecedents, presumably to establish a causality that will influence our perceptions of his own case:

> El deseo que tenía—curioso lector—de contarte mi vida, me daba tanta priesa para engolfarte en ella sin prevenir algunas cosas que, como

primer principio, es bien dejallas entendidas—porque siendo esenciales a este discurso también te serán no de pequeño gusto—que me olvidaba de cerrar un portillo por donde me entrara cualquier terminista acusando de mal latín, redarguyéndome de pecado, porque no procedí de la difinición a lo difinido y antes de contarla no dejé dicho quiénes y cuáles fueron mis padres y confuso nacimiento.... (I, 1, 1: 99–100)

[The desire that I had, curious reader, to tell you my life made me hurry so to engulf you in it, without advising of certain things that, at the very beginning, it is best to leave understood—because, being essential to this discourse, they also will be of no small pleasure to you—that I forgot to close a little opening that might invite any pedant to accuse me of poor letters, impugning me for sinning, since I didn't proceed from the definition to the defined, and before telling my life I didn't make clear who and which were my parents and confused birth....]

The first chapter dedicated to clarification of such particulars, however, stages a series of diversionary tactics reminiscent of the trial defense of a known criminal (Cascardi, "Rhetoric of Defense," 382; Woods, "Teasing Opening of the *Guzmán*," 217–18). Chapter 1 makes no reference to the crimes in which Guzmán may have been schooled. Instead we learn of his progenitors' influential status: "Vinieron a residir a Génoa, donde fueron agregados a la nobleza" [They came to reside in Genoa, where they were accepted into the company of nobility] (I, 1, 1: 105–6) and find that his father sported the latest of fashion: "Era blanco, rubio, colorado, rizo, y creo de naturaleza tenía los ojos grandes, turquesados. Traía copete y sienes ensortijadas" [He was white, blond, rosy, with ringlets, and I believe that his eyes were naturally large, turquoise colored. He sported a forelock and curly temples] (I, 1, 1: 118).[27] Guzmán's predecessors enjoyed the life that Alemán has hinted the narrator will seek for himself—as "agregados a la nobleza" (attached to the nobility) they were, in effect, "accepted as courtiers." Their vices, we learn—from usury to makeup—reflected those of the nobility whose lifestyle they shared (I: 106). Just as his relatives' unsavory service at Court gave them license to indulge in expressions of deviancy that illustrious men permitted themselves, similarly, Guzmán, who confesses, takes liberty in mimicking the subversion of testimony practiced by justice officials swayed by bribes. He introduces his own case as the account primarily of the wrongs of the system responsible for his sentencing, listing the falsehoods and self-interest of magistrates, scribes, and judges (I, 1, 1: 111–17). By parodying the verbal authority of his judges with the circumlocutions of his oratory, he reveals their words to be no more reliable than his own discourse. The logical relationship that Guzmán establishes between deviancy in which his family—as "hangers-on"—has complied, and deviancy practiced by those (nobility and ministers of justice) charged with ordering society and providing its models for behavior, reflects far more negatively on the latter, we note, than on the accused.[28] The shifting perspectives of Guzmán's reasoning work to establish either familial honor for him or the dishonor of his social superiors and judges. By multiplying with the language of his narration the definitions of honor, Guzmán both prepares us for the pluralism of his discourse and for one of the novel's primary themes: pursuit of the favor from "illustrious men" that constitutes social honor.[29]

The narrator keeps our attention fixed upon his act of narration after this initial frame by continuing to confuse his avowed intentions or the "difinición" while he tells his story, or "difinido." He manipulates the way in which the narrative conveys its message so overtly that readers cannot overlook his authorial role. Guzmán states that he will relate his life as a *pícaro* in order to provide a negative example so that readers will be able to form their own judgments about deception. But he halts the syntagmatic development of his story frequently in order to interpret the narrated material for them. Readers are told how the *pícaro*'s actions should be judged in digressions that include moral discourses, sermons, anecdotes, allegories, and even four Italianate *novellas*. In these segments of advice the narrator repeatedly shifts focus away from his own culpable activities, displacing himself as the subject under discussion. Guzmán attributes his deceptiveness to others and becomes a social critic; he allegorizes his behavior, offering philosophical commentary; or he theorizes on the deception of language that affects social communication as it is exemplified by the lives of characters in other stories. In the process, readers tend to forget what has been happening in the main narrative of Guzmán's own duplicity.

The narrator's shifts of perspective have frustrated modern critics in search of his "point of view,"[30] but as Smith argues (*Writing in the Margin*, 105), literary precepts of Alemán's time did not include a psychologically unified or "pictorial" depiction of subjectivity.[31] Rather than being artistic accidents, the fragmented views that we receive of Guzmán, who—the title to Part II tells us specifically—addresses readers as "atalaya de la vida humana" (the watchtower of human life), have the important function of displacing reader attention from the individual who narrates onto the relationships that his language establishes between him and society. Guzmán's gaze represents spatially the power that language gives him to alter the positions of himself and his readers—both vertically and horizontally, as Chapters 2 and 3 will demonstrate—in the world that he creates.[32] Smith observes (109) that in creating Guzmán's discourse, Alemán anticipates the "panoptisme," or investigatory examination from one controlling locus of a multitude of subjects, examined by Foucault in *Surveiller et punir* (*Discipline and Punish*):

> We might see the *Guzmán* (like the panopticon) as a laboratory which serves to fragment and magnify human productivity: in each tiny incident (each graphically illuminated cell) the subject is 'caught' in a posture which requires praise or blame, reward or punishment. In its role as witness, the readership holds a privileged position. The multitude is made visible to the single person in a spectacle of surveillance: we observe Guzmán, who is aware of his own visibility. As I suggested earlier, the critic's gaze is often inquisitorial: we are tempted to make 'empirical' judgements as to the 'facts' of Guzmán's case.

Perhaps more accurately, Alemán's writing parodies the interrogatory model of his own time that was precursor to the Enlightenment's later version of centralized observation and correction—the Inquisition. Analyzing the language through which Guzmán is made to "confess" to invisible superiors as if he were on the stand, while simultaneously articulating their judgments, Cros ("Predication carcérale," 72) characterizes the narrator's discourse as a hybrid of the voice of the criminal or "true subject" and that of an inquisitor, representing a collective process of censorship and discipline.[33] I would have to dispute Smith's contention, however, that the narration through which Guzmán tells his lifestory gives the reader a "privileged position," as well as the argument of Cros that the voice of the narrative's subject is repressed by the collective force of the dominant ideology to which he pays homage. The existence and power of repressive norms is acknowledged by his self-castigating discourse. But Guzmán's expression of compliance with authority is supplemented with a challenge to the fixity of its norms, in the refusal to limit the scope of his words to univocity. Brancaforte (*¿Conversión o proceso de degradación?*, 140) argues that in Guzmán's narrative, the process of "self-flagellation" is inseparable from that of "whipping the readers." In fact, he maintains, Guzmán's self-contradictory religious argumentation and the linguistic structures used to support it reveal that the narrator's words "sirven para empequeñecer ... el mensaje del sermón" [serve to diminish ... the sermon's message]. He adds:

Esto no puede ser casual, ni fruto de la inocencia del protagonista–narrador, sino que debe de corresponder a un deseo consciente de "inficionar" la teoría predicada en el sermón de perdón y del amor cristiano.

[This cannot be fortuitous, nor a product of the protagonist-narrator's innocence, but rather must correspond to a conscious desire to "contaminate" the theory preached in the sermon of forgiveness and Christian love.]

Indeed, the meaning of *atalaya* in *germanía* (thieves' cant), Guzmán's own tongue, warns of the subversive use that the narrator may make of his shifting vantage point. *Diccionario de autoridades* records *atalaya* (s.v.) as also meaning "thief" in *germanía*. In narrating his life, Guzmán may rob readers of their worth.

Readers are invited to view the behavior of Guzmán under surveillance, but the surveillance is his own. In producing the truth about himself, he usurps their vantage point, directing the view of so-called "prudent readers" with a polyvalence that is ultimately subject to the designs of his monologue. Arguing that "autobiography is one of the most limited forms in terms of perspective," Arias points out (*Unrepentant Narrator*, 2, 3) that "our dependence upon Guzmán, galley-slave-cum-religious convert, is absolute," even in the numerous digressions of his narrative that appear intended to give a more comprehensive view of his character.[34] Guzmán also avails himself of the watchtower or *atalaya* from which he speaks to survey the deviant behavior of others and to record its need of correction.[35] Ironically, the mobility of the discourse through which he composes his account enables Guzmán the criminal to move from a marginal position as either a *pícaro desechado* (ostracized rogue) or *admitido* (one accepted) under suspicion, to one of power, as an authoritative voice whose figure the accused never clearly see. For in shifting perspectives as well as discursive registers, the process of Guzmán's narration makes it impossible for readers to assemble a coherent figure. As Barros warned (I: 93), we are confronted in his self-representation with the "inevitable contradiction of the diversity of views." Readers see all—and yet only—what Guzmán's words depict, and the judgments they find are his.

In addition to highlighting his narrative deceptiveness by shifting the object of his narration frequently, Guzmán warns us explicitly in several places that his didactic intentions are true, but that the language through which they are articulated structures itself on what appear to be lies. In the beginning of Part I we find that the narrator's "hábito," or means of representing himself, will brand him linguistically as a *pícaro* (I, 2, 3: 271).

By offering advice to his betters through his chosen discourse, the narrator admits that he will be identified by the *vulgo* ("alguno del arte mercante") as a fool, a convicted criminal, and a shiftless trickster, whose appropriation of the authoritative discourse of his judges constitutes, as well as their edification, a serious transgression: "Alguno del arte mercante me dirá: «. . . ¿Quién mete al idiota, galeote, pícaro, en establecer leyes ni calificar los tratos que no entiende?»" [Someone of the mercantile art will doubtlessly say to me: ". . . Who is putting an idiot, galley slave, a rogue, up to establishing laws and assessing dealings that he does not understand?"] (I, 1, 1: 110). In so doing he makes it clear that readers should not overlook his present straits as a galley slave, for they affect the way in which he speaks. Not simply a pious penitent, but one who has converted in close proximity to the gallows steps, Guzmán will not hesitate to make the language of his narration serve his ends. Guzmán begins to suggest a plurality of functions for himself that may account for the shifting registers of his narration: in addition to his new function as *homo litteratus* in the composition of an autobiography through which he hopes to win favor, he speaks both as a presumptuous fool and a hardened deceiver. The narrator goes on to highlight his mental alacrity in the second book of Part I and then, as will be discussed later in this chapter, he examines his function as a "clever fool" at the novel's center, in Part I, Book 3 and Part II, Book 1.

Guzmán tells us in I, 2 that although he presents his private history as a confession, it is within his power as narrator to control the way that damaging information about himself is divulged. While he explicitly criticizes some of his exemplary wrongs in digressions, the narrator admits to readers his unwillingness to discuss others or his outright suppression of them: "Quiero callar y no habrá ley contra mí: mi secreto para mí, que al buen callar llaman santo" [I wish to remain silent and there's no law against it: my secret is for me alone, for they call prudent silence sacred] (I, 2, 3: 276). Guzmán suggests that his readers should be wary of his discourse by depicting their reactions to his process of narration:

> Preguntarásme: «¿Dónde va Guzmán tan cargado de ciencia? ¿Qué piensa hacer con ella? ¿Para qué fin la loa con tan largas arengas y engrandece con tales veras? ¿Qué nos quiere decir? ¿Adónde ha de parar?»
> Por mi fee, hermano mío, a dar con ella en un esportón, que fue la ciencia que estudié para ganar de comer, que es una buena parte della;

pues quien ha oficio ha beneficio y el que otro no sabía para pasar la vida, tanto lo estimé para mí en aquel tiempo, como en el suyo Demóstenes la elocuencia y sus astucias Ulixes. (I, 2, 7: 317)

[You will ask me: "Where is Guzmán headed so full of erudition? What does he plan to do with it? To what end does he praise it in such long-winded arguments and exalt it with such truths? What does he wish to tell us? Where will it end?"
By my faith, brother mine, to land with it in a big basket, which was the first skill I studied to earn my bread, which is a good part of it; for he who has an office has a benefice and as one who knew no other means by which to live, I held it in as much esteem at that time as did Demosthenes eloquence in his and Ulysses his wiles.]

He acknowledges that his self-critical narrative is organized by the same acquired knowledge—a principle of communication—that informed his behavior as a *pícaro*. The narrator equates this "science" with classical rhetoric and Ulysses's wiles. Readers are alerted to the fact that in allowing Guzmán to speak indirectly or figuratively, his medium also enables him to conceal his objectives, if he so desires. We are reminded of Alemán's opening allusions to the narrator's private goals and Barros's warnings regarding the multiple facets through which this figure will depict himself. The case that motivates Guzmán's confession, however, does not receive explicit discussion by the galley slave until Part II, and then it is divulged slowly.

In Part II, Chapter 1, Guzmán cryptically retorts that he need not have become a "penitent" to achieve the additional aim of "lo que más aquí pretendo" [what else I am after here] (II, 1, 1: 36). He then quickly denies a second objective by arguing that all along his only intent has been to help the readers avoid his fate:

La mía ya te dije que sólo era de tu aprovechamiento, de tal manera que puedas con gusto y seguridad pasar por el peligroso golfo del mar que navegas. Yo aquí recibo los palos y tú los consejos en ellos. Mía es la hambre y para ti la industria, como no la padezcas. Yo sufro las afrentas de que nacen tus honras. (II, 1, 1: 36–37)

[Mine, I already told you, was only for your benefit, so that you may with pleasure and safety pass through the dangerous gulf of the sea you sail. Here I receive the beatings and you the admonishment in them. Mine is the hunger and for you the hard work, so that you will not undergo it. I suffer the affronts from which your honors are born.]

But he undermines the accuracy of the second assertion, stating enigmatically that he may in fact be telling the truth or lies: "O te digo verdades o mentiras" (II: 37). A few pages later, Guzmán finally begins to explain his private motives for writing. We find that he is anxious to have his life as a character prolonged so that he may continue his work as an author.

We receive the first explanation of why the narrator expects that his end is near. Guzmán expresses fear that while he languishes in chains, someone else may "finish him off" by publishing a spurious third part to his autobiography. Voicing Alemán's derision of the illegitimate Part II written by Juan Martí between his own two volumes,[36] Guzmán begs that he not be "hanged" by this other writer. He claims that he merits further life in order to complete his self-emendation and to write his own Part III:

> La verdadera mía iré prosiguiendo, aunque más me vayan persiguiendo. Y no faltará otro Gil para la tercera parte, que me arguya como en la segunda de lo que nunca hice, dije ni pensé. Lo que le suplico es que no tome tema ni tanta cólera comigo, que me ahorque por su gusto, que ni estoy en tiempo dello ni me conviene. Déjeme vivir, pues Dios ha sido servido de darme vida en que me corrija y tiempo para la enmienda. Servirán aquí mis penas para escusarte dellas, informándote para que sepas encadenar lo pasado y presente con lo venidero de la tercera parte y que, hecho de todo un trabado contexto, quedes cual debes, instruido en las veras. (II, 1, 1: 42–43)

> [My own true one I will continue on with, although they may still pursue me. Another Gil will not likely be missing to pen a third part, who will impugn me, as in the (spurious) second one, for what I never did, said, or thought. What I beseech of you is that you neither bear me a grudge nor so much anger that you hang me at your pleasure, for neither am I ready for it nor does it suit me. Let me live, since God has seen fit to give me life in which to correct myself and time for emendation. My punishments here will serve to exempt you from them, informing you so that you will know how to link the past and present with that which is forthcoming in the third part, and that, with all made one unified context, you will be left as you should be, instructed in the truths.]

The request that Guzmán be allowed to live on, however, is not simply a joke upon Alemán's rival. The narrator's request that he be spared death is motivated from within the narrative, although we are not made aware of it until we have read almost all of Guzmán's account. Some nine hundred pages into the novel, we find in its last two chapters (II, 3, 8–9) that after Guzmán has been made a galley slave for his crimes and after his alleged religious conversion, he has been compromised in a mutinous conspiracy of slaves aboard ship, although he defends his cooperation with them as involuntary. In an attempt to solve the problem to his superiors' and presumably his own advantage, he has informed on the others. The conspirators have been punished or executed by various methods—one is by hanging (II, 3, 9: 479). Guzmán claims that he, however, was exonerated and promised reward ("todo buen galardón") by the ship's captain upon arrival of "His Majesty's decree" (II, 3, 9: 480). Nevertheless, as the novel ends, we find that he still awaits this verification of his safety: "me mandó desherrar y que como libre anduviese por la galera, en cuanto venía cédula de Su Majestad, en que absolutamente lo mandase, porque así se lo suplicaban y lo enviaron consultado" [he ordered me unshackled and to be allowed to go about the galley as if freed as soon as His Majesty's decree should arrive, in which it would be absolutely ordered, because they were requesting this of him and sent it for his consideration] (II: 480).[37] Recalling Alemán's statement at the beginning of Part I that his character was composing a narrative for presentation "on the gallows steps," we must assume that Guzmán is in danger of being hanged as a co-conspirator. He appears uncertain that a royal decree authorizing commutation of his sentence will actually be issued. In his anxiety to guarantee this response, so vital not merely to his freedom from chains but perhaps also to his freedom from death, Guzmán presents his own testimony in the form of an autobiographical novel.

Guzmán attempts to argue persuasively that he merits further life by creating a personal account that plays down his responsibility for the deceptions exemplified therein, including the recent plot of mutiny, and which portrays him to be morally regenerated. Although Guzmán's status as a galley slave prevents him from directly addressing this recipient, he implicitly offers his autobiography to the King, who is the master of royal galley slaves and has the power either to intervene in Guzmán's case with a decree of commutation or to allow the character to be hanged by the ship's captain along with the other conspirators. While he has been promised a reward as an informant by the ship's captain, Guzmán's description, immediately preceding, of the captain's antipathy toward him implies considerable doubt that such a decree will be carried out, should it be granted. The narrator cites an earlier situation in which he was framed in the theft of a gold-trimmed hatband from the captain's relative and punished mercilessly by the latter although his guilt had not been verified. He observes that the captain would have tortured him to death but did not want to pay the King his due for the unwarranted loss of an able-bodied slave:

> Mandáronme dar azotes de muerte; mas temiéndose ya el capitán que me quedaba poco para perder la vida y que me había de pagar al rey, si allí peligrase, tuvo a partido que se perdiese antes el trencellín que perderlo y pagarme. (II, 3, 9: 474)

> [They ordered me to be given death lashes; however the captain, fearing that I was already on the verge of dying and that he would have to pay the King for me if that risk was run there, decided that it was for the better simply to lose the hatband than both to lose it and to have to pay for me.]

Guzmán adds that the captain continued to harbor malice toward him and punished him excessively even for minor infractions of the rules (II: 475). The convict-turned-author appears to be worried that the circumstances of his final dilemma cause him to be "framed" in "apparent" wrongdoing again, this time in a situation that gives the captain justification for executing him. In making a public record of his undeserved mistreatment at the hands of the captain, Guzmán implies that the latter's violation of regulations governing the treatment of galley slaves might well draw the interest and perhaps intervention of their owner. Like his predecessor, Lázaro, this narrator hopes to deflect some of the blame that will otherwise befall him onto his superior, a subordinate of the account's real destinary. As an author, Guzmán, like Alemán, thus addresses his literary work both to one implied *discreto*, whose status as judge he would like to replace with that of patron. Guzmán also generalizes the designation to a class of readers, who he hopes will praise his altruism in both revealing the recent plot of mutiny and admitting to his own crimes. By granting his novel acclaim, *discretos* are able to do more than prolong Guzmán's temporal existence; they are able to immortalize him.

Not until the end of the novel do we fully comprehend that there is in fact no temporal distinction between Guzmán the character and Guzmán the narrator; they are one and the same. As a character Guzmán tries to assure that his temporal life will be spared by speaking with guile, and as a narrator he also seeks the more lasting existence conferred through renown by cleverly conveying moral and political lessons. Only after we have read through his account do the narrator's statements about his present function at the beginning of Part II take on their full meaning. In order to achieve the private, self-serving objective of currying favor with readers in order to avoid further punishment himself, and his publicly-proclaimed, apparently altruistic purpose of helping them to reform their own misguided behavior, Guzmán tells us that he supplements his authorial or "watchtower" role with that of a particular type of professional trickster. He is no longer a street *pícaro*, whose deceptions are expressed in harmful actions such as swindles and thefts. He now lives by his *pico*, or mouth, as a literary jester or wise fool.[38] The narrator voices criticisms of his masters indirectly by ridiculing his own behavior, affirming their superiority while he entertains, so that he may dispose them positively toward his desires. Yet with the daring of the foolhardy he boldly harangues them in countless digressions for faults worse than his own. In so doing, he invokes his experience as a jester and a comic for audiences of *discretos* within the story. At the end of Part I and the beginning of Part II, the narrator reveals to us that the two most prestigious, successful jobs of his past as a *pícaro* were ones in which he was able to trade his street rags for the livery of society by becoming a court jester. While he explains his previous work as jester, the narrator also tells us ways in which his present function is analogous, as Rodríguez has pointed out (*El narrador pícaro*, 71–92; "La poética del gracioso," 403–12).

After describing a series of jobs in which he learned how to live by deception at the margins of society as a boy, the narrator ends Part I by explaining that his skills as a trickster eventually brought him social acceptance and limited material security in two jobs as a court jester or buffoon. He highlights his function as a buffoon not only by positioning it at mid-point in the novel, but also by giving it far more attention than he does to his other jobs as a *pícaro*. Most of Part I consists of short chapters that include the description of one job plus digression. In the final section, however, Guzmán devotes three chapters to the description his wiles as a false beggar that led to his first position as a jester (I, 3, 2–4). He then ends Part I with an account of his work as a court buffoon that spans four chapters (I, 3, 7–10). Although these sections will be discussed in further detail in the next chapter of this study, brief reference to them here will help to clarify this important facet of the narrator's figure.

We learn that Guzmán was formerly a jester and comic for two prominent masters: a Roman cardinal and the French ambassador to Rome. Guzmán's convincing appearance of misery as a false beggar caused the cardinal to pity him in I, 3, 6 and the *pícaro* was taken into the latter's service to be a page. However, he quickly distinguished himself from the other pages by demonstrating superior conceptual wit in tricks and pranks—*burlas*—which he played on members of the household. Guzmán tells us that no one was safe from his wiles. He embarrassed and annoyed other servants by making them the victims of serious practical jokes (*burlas pesadas*) that caused material harm or damaged their reputations, causing them to fear him: "La burla se solemnizó más que la primera.... Desta vez quedé confirmado por quien era: todos huían de mis burlas como del pecado" [This joke had more serious effects than the first.... From this time forth I was confirmed for who I really was: everyone fled my jokes as from sin itself] (I, 3, 8: 436). The narrator Guzmán boasts that he even dared to play jokes on the cardinal by performing innocent *burlas* or *tropelías*—sleight of hand tricks—in his presence. Both the *burlas pesadas* and Guzmán's less serious *burlas* served to entertain the cardinal and to bring Guzmán public acclaim in this position. His master took such pleasure in these examples of deception that Guzmán was elevated to the privileged position of household wit or jester (I, 3, 9: 445).

The narrative describes Guzmán's education in the first part of the *trivium*, or grammar, under the cardinal's employment (I: 445). Besides developing his linguistic abilities in Latin, Greek, and Hebrew, Guzmán becomes skilled in types of deception particularly well suited to the cultured society of *discretos*. In addition to learning to perform *tropelías*, tricks that deceive the eyes of the beholder—which anticipate Guzmán's confusion later when performing as a watchtower of the readers' view of him—Guzmán also learns how to narrate pleasing stories and play games (I, 3, 9: 446).

When Guzmán is dismissed from the cardinal's service for gambling, he then enters the service of the French ambassador to Rome (I, 3, 10: 454). We learn that Guzmán continued to perform as a buffoon for this new master by playing both instructive and harmful *burlas* upon victims, according to the whims of the ambassador. For example, he revealed the hypocrisies of dinner guests publicly and he tricked Roman matrons into compromising liaisons with his master. The description of his second job as jester begins in the final chapter of Part I and resumes at the opening of Part II, where it fills most of the first book—a third of the volume. The narrator explains that his pranks often backfired, harming him more than the intended victims, because they were poorly conceived or executed. He possessed insufficient "letras" or further education in the *trivium*—rhetoric and logic, we must assume—which might have enabled him to play jokes upon others through a more complex presentation. And he showed his audience to be guilty of culpable as well as ridiculous behavior. The narrator Guzmán tells us that therefore he was unable to win the audience response that he now acknowledges to be an important objective of every professional jester—that of their good will and predisposition to reward him (II, 1, 2: 49). In fact, he was forced to resign his position as jester when one of his poorly executed pranks caused the ambassador to be publicly humiliated.

Before resuming the account of his work for the French ambassador at the beginning of Part II, the narrator introduces the volume with an explanation of his method. He uses the first chapter of his second volume, entitled "Guzmán de Alfarache disculpa el proceso de su discurso, pide atención y da noticia de su intento" ("Guzmán apologizes for the procedure of his discourse, requests attention, and informs of his intent"), to direct our reading of his narration. And in so doing, he mirrors Alemán's "Declaración" at the beginning of Part I. Guzmán observes that readers will judge his narrative procedure to be daring to the point of being foolish, because in the course of his admonitions he "throws stones" or criticizes them apparently without worrying about repercussions (II, 1, 1: 35). He points out, however, that readers need not acknowledge the gravity of his charges against them, for although it appears threatening, the irony of his language renders his critical discourse unreliable: "Hablando voy a ciegas y dirásme muy bien que estoy muy cerca de hablar a tontas . . ." [Speaking, I'm casting in the dark, and you might very well say that I'm nearly speaking nonsense . . .] (II, 1, 1: 35). In order to censure the readers' behavior and yet manipulate them into responding to him with favor, Guzmán must present a critical message that appears to be discountable, he must draw the readers' attention away from the criticism leveled at themselves, and he must entertain them.

With customary guile, the narrator tells us that he has chosen the role that he knows from experience is the most effective for these purposes: he has begun once again to function as a clever joker or pretentious fool—a "figura," as Barros warned—who gives readers the satisfaction of being able to ridicule him while he threatens their complacency. He has already admitted to us in the narrative of Part I that his deceptions as a jester enabled him to humiliate victims and to exact special privileges from his superiors. Therefore, the narrator Guzmán admits his manipulative capabilities in this role only with great reluctance. He acknowledges that by the present time he may have remedied educational deficiencies that limited the effectiveness of his *burlas* before. And yet he leads us to think that he dare not play jokes on us in narrating because the personal stakes have become too high for him. But Guzmán then proceeds to reveal an analogy between his present function as narrator and his previous one as comic or jester so that readers will not be ignorant of the possibility of "jokes" or discursive deception in his present narration:

> Y si dijeres que hago ascos de mi propio trato, que te lo vendo caro haciéndome de rogar o que hago melindre, pesaráme que lo juzgues a tal. Que, aunque es notoria verdad haber servido siempre a el embajador, mi señor, de su gracioso, entonces pude, aunque no supe, y, aunque agora supiese, no puedo, porque tienen mucha costa y no todo tiempo es uno. Mas, para que no ignores lo que digo y sepas cuáles eran mis gracias entonces y lo que agora sería necesario para ellas, oye con atención el capítulo siguiente. (II, 1, 1: 44–45)
>
> [And if you say that I turn up my nose at my own behavior, that I sell it to you dearly wanting to be coaxed or that I feign affectation, it will grieve me that you so judge it. For, although my having always served the ambassador, my lord, as his comic is a well-known fact, then I managed to do so, although I didn't know how, and, even though now I might know how, I cannot, for jokes are costly and times are different. Yet, so that you will not overlook what I say and so that you may know the nature of my jests then and what now would be necessary for them, listen carefully to the following chapter.]

In Part II, Book 1, Chapter 2, Guzmán demonstrates that jesters in fact have a beneficial purpose in society. He observes that such figures are indispensable to rulers and politicians as discreet advisers, because they can be counted upon to deliver messages of truth without giving offense, by communicating figurally—with verbal wit and physical representation.[39] The narrator draws our attention to his experience both as a joker and an adviser: "Necesario es y tanto suele a veces importar un buen chocarrero, como el mejor consejero . . . de uno y otro tengo experiencia" [A good comic is necessary and at times is as important as the best counselor . . . I have experience at both] (II, 1, 2: 47).[40] Guzmán goes on to describe three types of jester (II, 1, 2: 50–53) and four classes of *burla* (II, 1, 3: 63–68), which are defined according to their effects on the public. We find that, according to Guzmán's definitions, in his present act of narration he may be characterized as a *juglar discreto*, or fool who discreetly communicates advice, and we find reassurances that the deceptive medium of his language does not play with readers' perceptions for the purpose of harming them. The narrator Guzmán voices Alemán's stated intent to offer politic advice to the readers in the guise of the only speaker from whom they are likely to accept it—the jester, whose words are publicly discountable:

Esto he venido a decir, porque de mí no se sienta que quiero contravenir a que los príncipes tengan en sus casas hombres de placer o juglares. Y no sería malo cuando los tuviesen tanto para su entretenimiento, cuanto para recoger por aquel arcaduz algunas cosas, que no les entraría bien por otro. Y éstos, acontecen ocasiones en que suelen valer mucho, advirtiendo, aconsejando, revelando cosas graves en son de chocarrerías, que no se atrevieran cuerdos a decirlas con veras.

Graciosos hay discretos, que dicen sentencias y dan pareceres que no se humillaran sus amos a pedirlos a otros de sus criados, aunque les importaran mucho y fueran ellos grandísimos estadistas para poderles aconsejar, ni lo consintieran dellos, por no confesarse ignorantes a sus inferiores o que saben menos que ellos; que aun hasta en esto quieren ser dioses. Y estos criados tales eran los papagayos que deseaba tener Júpiter enjaulados. Que no es de agora el daño ni nació ayer despreciar los consejos de los tales poderosos. (II, 1, 2: 50)

[I have come to tell you this, because I do not want it felt of me that I am opposed to princes having men of pleasure or jesters in their employ. And it would not be wrong when they had them as much for their entertainment as to gather through that conduit some things that wouldn't enter their attention well by any other. And these jesters, there are times when they are worth a great deal, warning, advising, revealing serious matters that sound like jokes, which the prudent would not dare to utter in truth.

There are prudent jesters, who pronounce judgments and give opinions that their masters would not humiliate themselves to ask of their other servants, even though they might matter greatly and the servants might be great statesmen in their abilities to advise them, nor would they consent to it from them, so as to not confess themselves ignorant to their inferiors or that they know less than they; for even in this they wish to be gods. And these same servants were the parrots that Jupiter wished to have caged. For the harm in this does not date from present times, nor did the disdaining of advice on the part of the powerful begin only yesterday.]

The narrator uses the self-representation of his autobiography to create a harmless deception—an ingenious literary discourse that catalogues the criminal and immoral deceptions of one who, while a favored wit, comes from outside their social milieu. Prudent readers are to find benefit and pleasure in Guzmán's representations and will not be misled by the instability of his narrative discourse in the way that they might suffer deception from the actions of an ordinary *pícaro*. Instead, they will consider his literary performance to be an entertaining deception:

La tercera manera de engaños es cuando son sin perjuicio, que ni engañan a otro con ellos ni lo quedan los que quieren o tratan de engañar. Lo cual es en dos maneras: o con obras o palabras. Palabras, contando cuentos, refieriéndo novelas, fábulas y otras cosas de entretenimiento; y obras, como son las del juego de manos y otros primores o tropelías que se hacen y son sin algún daño ni perjuicio de tercero. (II, 1, 3: 66)

[The third manner of deceptions is when they are without prejudice, for they neither deceive another with them nor are those who wish to or attempt to deceive left themselves deceived. That manner is in two ways: either with acts or words. Words, telling stories, narrating novellas, fables, and other things of entertainment; and acts, such as are those of the sleight of hand and other skills or tricks that are done and are without any harm or prejudice to a third party.]

In tracing the relationship between deception and falsehood, however, Guzmán warns that their difference is imperceptible. Deception (*engaño*) is defined as the skillful process that suppresses the distinction between dissimilar, even opposite senses. The danger of deception is precisely the pleasure it produces in its victims: the latter are allowed to form judgments that suit their desires, but which will ultimately result in their harm. Guzmán's terms signal the perceptual difficulties that will characterize his own discourse: "engaño" is "una red sutilísima" (a very subtle net), "imperceptible" (imperceptible) (II: 63), and "artificiosa" (artful) (II: 64), which "como áspide, mata con un sabroso sueño" (like an asp, kills with a delicious sleep) (II: 64). Perfect examples of deception lie in Guzmán's restless gaze upon facets of himself and his society, and in the shifting discursive registers that accompany his own brand of "panoptisme," for readers are responsible for assembling not only that "defined" by his autobiography or the facts of his life, but also the "definition" or standards by which to judge it. As the narrator both entertains and advises them with his deceptive account, readers who comprise the general, undiscerning public will become deceived (*burlados*), or will be taken in, with pleasure.

We are also made to suspect that Guzmán continues his past work as a self-interested joker, whose use of the deception of language in communicating both yielded profit at the expense of his victims and in turn handed him a life—or perhaps death—sentence as a galley slave. He has emphasized the importance of capturing the goodwill ("captar la benevolencia"), conquering the tastes ("rindiendo los gustos") of the audience to his ends, but has refused to delimit those intentions to one that is clearly delineated ("cierto fin y determinado"), by which we may interpret the act of offering his story in order to respond to it. Guzmán vacillates between the role of a well-intentioned prudent jester and that of what might be termed an indiscreet joker, as he exercises his power to humiliate publicly in order to pursue the self-serving ends of winning freedom from his civil sentence and fame as a man of letters.[41] As I have cited previously, Rodríguez (*El narrador pícaro*, 86) suggests with sharp insight that the narrating *pícaro* attempts to strike a deal with the reader: witticisms for pardon ("gracias a cambio de la gracia"). That is, Guzmán seeks to exchange his jokes for favor.

In describing the fourth class of deception—that of the *burlador burlado* or "the deceiver himself deceived"—the narrator Guzmán relates an anecdote that mirrors his relationship with the readers. In this example, a court poet finds that his role as an entertainer has been usurped by the prince for whom he writes. The latter has grown tired of being obliged to favor the poet's offerings of literary artifice and has decided to rid himself of the poet by humiliating him. The prince indicates that he no longer has need of the poet by composing his own sonnet and offering it to him. However, the poet proves to be the more competent master of deception. He merely reaches into his pocket and in public view rewards the prince's genius, representing the response that the prince should have produced as a reader in the first place. His reader the prince is left the butt of a joke that he thought he controlled (II, 1, 3: 66–67).

As he teaches us about social use and abuse of the power inherent in the figural potential of language by exposing his own deceptive narrations, the narrator Guzmán does not make himself a victim of his own ridicule out of unmotivated altruism. With its contradictory, shifting perspectives, his self-representation as watchtower of human nature traces unmistakably the response of favor that he desires from readers for not individuating them more clearly in his gaze upon examples of deception that harm society. The figure who narrates willingly depicts in himself all their foibles; in fact, through the multiple discourses that he articulates he mirrors those whom he views—from convict, moralist, wheeler-dealer, philosopher, penitent, and ingratiating servant to confidence man. In fragmenting our view of himself, Guzmán frustrates readers' desires to define him and thereby to circumscribe the influence of his deceptive language upon them by interpreting it in the proper context. Perhaps more disconcerting than the inconsistencies of his personality are the doubts readers must harbor about the position of Guzmán relative to their own. While his words represent society, Guzmán the convict's narration underscores the fundamental mutability of all relationships in language. His autobiography constitutes a potent warning to society of a "self-made man," that the discourses with which it seeks to define and punish deviation will not, by the nature of their composition, sustain themselves as autonomous structures—man's relationships in language are contextual, as are the material ones it defines. As a prudent jester who censures their wrongs by ridiculing his own and an indiscreet joker who implicitly demands reward for so doing, the narrating *pícaro* attempts to profit by literary expiation, thereby securing responses of favor that will transform his present state of material dishonor into the lasting honor of a renowned author. Whether his linguistic existence will liberate him from the material one from which it is said to arise rests with the reception of the book by its *discreto lector*.

2
Guzmán's History

The attention that his words draw to themselves in the opening lines of I, 1, 1 (99–100), clearly identifies Guzmán de Alfarache's autobiography as a study in the power of language to establish identity. This beginning, which directs interpretation of the narrative to follow, thwarts the process of signification declared proper by *terministas* (authorities in procedures of argumentation): signifiers, or *difiniciones*, articulated by the present discourse of Alemán's narrator, do not guarantee univocal meaning to the signifieds, or *difinidos*, that the narrative of his past represents. In the description of his progenitors, the stubborn refusal of the narrator's discourse to yield a clear assessment of his social and moral heritage highlights the precarious dependency of his figure—and our perceptions—upon the language that creates it. As he begins the story of his life, Guzmán's unreliable authorial utterances assume the tone of serious, learned discourse, but the true idiom of his narration is the *burla*, or joke, for readers will be teased if not tricked by the multiple interpretations they are invited to make of his beginnings.

Readers have been forewarned by Alemán in the Introduction that Guzmán's language is intended to produce social identity, situating him alternately near the gallows—as a "desechado" (one rejected)— and among courtiers—as an "admitido" (one who is accepted). The terms of reference through which Guzmán does so, however, do not find clear definition in his narration. The narrating *pícaro* who parodies scholars has chosen to invert the rules by which they play. After devoting two chapters to the baiting of readers with thwarted definitions of his family, Guzmán turns us over to the narrative and the content defined therein. Our assessment of the discourse of his narration, we find, will be informed by the text of the narrative. While the former—composed as a directed monologue—denies us the temporal distance and social context necessary for understanding the function of Guzmán's language until the two temporal planes converge in the novel's final pages, the narrative of past experience represents a historical dimension that exemplifies Guzmán's communication and its social effects quite clearly. The *difinidos*, or episodes of his lifestory, model the procedure of his *difinición*, or manner of telling it, but they are deconstructed, step by step, as Guzmán's present narration is not.

While horizontal development of the novel claims to portray the narrator's life, representation of Guzmán's growth and maturation falls short of the realism that modern readers may seek to associate with the novel. The protagonist is chronicled from an early age to manhood, but episodes of the narrative provide scant personal detail with which to assemble a picture of him in the contexts described; appearance, specific age, habits, and the responses of others are glossed over quickly or left unclarified. Although the narrative intends to represent Guzmán's history, it is at the same time strangely achronic, for it positions readers' attention repeatedly on a particular mode of behavior, to the exclusion of other information, in the constitution of his character.[1] As Monique Joly argues (62–63), *burlas* are not simply used for entertaining effect in the narrative of the *Guzmán*; they form its basic structuring principle. The trajectory of the narrator's plights and triumphs, consisting of an extensive series of misleading communications that duplicate common structural elements while they increase in complexity, traces the process of his education as a professional trickster. The narrative thus represents metonymically Guzmán's formation as a "figure"—a figural entity and, as Barros's term warns in the Eulogy to Part I, an ambitious trickster—by projecting onto the text's temporal plane a portrayal of the manner in which he communicates, as he learns to compose his identity with language. The patterns of deception depicted in the narrative fulfill their exemplary function by encouraging readers to formulate critical responses to a concatenation of misleading contexts in which internal audiences, from Guzmanillo early on to his victims later, similarly struggle to decipher the rules underlying different examples of duplicitous communication. Readers enjoy an overview that their textual doubles lack, however, for the ironic distance of the narrative past allows them to witness the creation of the mimetic field that establishes each illusion and they may weigh the social effects of *burlas* upon fictive victims.[2]

Recipients or victims of deception within the novel are cast as either the general public or the prudent elite, but as textual examples discussed in this chapter will demonstrate, in practice the distinction disappears. The narrator praises the latter group for its ability to identify contexts of deception because he desires their favor, but we find that characters whose superior education and socio-economic status cause them to be desginated as "prudent" fall prey as readily to the enigmas of Guzmán's language as do members of the general public. The readers for whose function these two groups provide a metafictive mirroring face a double-edged challenge: they must organize and interpret an unwieldy corpus of information about the fictive *pícaro* and his ingenious deceptions, with the proviso explained in his narrative discourses, that they never imitate the communications he narrates. Yet despite this education in the *burlas* of language, they are made to suspect that as prudent readers the same fate of enchantment and embarrassment awaits them that has attended Guzmán's communications with other so-called "discretos" in the narrative. It is true that readers possess an overview of individual narrative examples, but subject to the principle of contiguity through which narratology structures the nature of Guzmán's existence as a "history," they are denied previous knowledge of the final case that directs the narrator's composition of the novel, his selection of information, and his language in conveying it. Like the audiences of Guzmán's communications within the text, even those readers who aspire to be "prudent" know little of the situation motivating his discourse until they reach the end of his account.

As the following chapter will explain, the polyvalence of the narration that organizes the writing of Guzmán's life is not explicitly deconstructed by the narrator; readers are intended to formulate their own analysis by comparing his present discourse with communications of his alleged past that duplicate or "anticipate," and thus highlight its principles. In this chapter, I will first seek to examine the portrait of Guzmán's representations of self within the narrative past. By reflecting the horizontal organization of Alemán's novel in my own sequential discussion of Guzmán's adventures, I may open myself to criticism for being insufficiently theoretical.[3] Nevertheless, it is my opinion that the metonymic development of the *Guzmán,* despite its repetitiveness, does have an important rhetorical function that is not evident unless Guzmán's communications are analyzed as a process. While the narrative is structured on a long series of *burlas,* or deceptions, Guzmán's—and through his example, the readers'—mastery of them is experiential and progresses through a series of refinements. The articulation of *burlas* is carefully adjusted to various audiences, and the changing context of Guzmán's communications indicates the social efficacy of language. As the narrator establishes his figure in the opening pages of the autobiography we receive indicators of his underlying social intentions that will take on fuller meaning when incorporated into the controlling framework laid out at the end of II, 3, 9, as Guzmán brings us up to the "present." Early lines of the convict-turned-author's case explain that from the beginning Guzmán has been inspired to live a life of deception by his desire to create a lasting appearance of "honor" for himself. The text thereby establishes one of the primary patterns of motivation for the communication through which the narrator represents himself in the novel's discourse.[4] Spurred on by this goal, Guzmán dedicates the mobility of his language to a search for the most profitable context in which to establish his presence.

In Part I, Book 1, Guzmán opens with a flourish of self-contradiction that readers quickly find to be a trademark of his language. First he tells us that he was predisposed to enter such a life of duplicity because his parents were *pícaros,* thereby awakening expectations of the social as well as moral determinism established long since in the famous *Lazarillo:*[5] for the protagonist we anticipate a life of economic hardship and thwarted aspirations to upward mobility.[6] Yet while the narrator encourages readers to deduce that as a boy he practiced deception simply to survive and to protect himself from the tricks of others, at the same time we are shown that "Guzmanillo" had ambitious plans for the use of his wiles even at an early age. Guzmán explains (I, 1, 2: 141) that upon his father's death, he entered the business of "entretenimientos, oficios, comisiones y otras cosas honrosas" [entertainments, offices, commissions, and other honorable things][7] and began to learn the skills of *picardía* to support himself and his mother, an aging prostitute. Admitting that he was able to provide adequately for their material needs, Guzmán remarks that the reduced social status associated with his work nevertheless conflicted with his personal sense of honor and dignity. The narrator points out, with what evidently is fine irony, that the "honradas partes" of his background caused him to feel that he merited a better future than life in the streets of Seville:[8]

> Yo fui desgraciado, como habéis oído: quedé solo, sin árbol que me hiciese sombra, los trabajos a cuestas, la carga pesada, las fuerzas flacas, la obligación mucha, la facultad poca. Ved si un mozo como yo, que ya galleaba, fuera justo con tan honradas partes estimarse en algo.
> El mejor medio que hallé fue probar la mano para salir de miseria, dejando mi madre y tierra. (I, 1, 2: 141–42)
>
> [I was unfortunate, as you have heard: I was left alone, without a tree to shade me, shouldering many tasks, the weight heavy, my strength weak, responsibility great, and my ability little. See if a boy like myself, who

already crowed, was right with such honorable parts to have a rather high opinion of himself.

The best means that I found was to try my hand at escaping the misery, leaving my mother and land.]

Whereas Lazarillo was thrust into the world of deception through his mother's rejection, Guzmanillo the *pícaro* eagerly abandons the maternal nest to prove not simply a newly gained sexual prowess, but more crucial to the enterprise of social ascent, to prove the potency of his rapidly maturing *pico*, evoked by the verb "galleaba." *Diccionario de autoridades*, s.v. *gallear*, explains that while the literal meaning of the verb is "tomar el gallo à las gallinas" (for the cock to mate with the hens), its figurative acceptation shifts focus: "Por alusión es querer sobresalir entre otros hablando . . ." [By allusion it is to wish to project an image or to stand out among others by speaking . . .]. Readers thus receive warning in these opening pages that the important locus of this narrator's power is his mouth: we soon find in the narrative that his control of the world surrounding him, as an implicit "cock," resides not in the literal force of sexuality but rather in the metaphoric potency of language.[9]

The chronicle of Guzmán's developing mastery of the society that seeks to restrict him through the aggressive reinterpretation of its realities with his *pico*, or mouth, is cloaked by synecdoche for most of Part I: the narrative places primary emphasis not on the mouth as the nexus for all sorts of communication with the outside world, but specifically on its material function in eating. The account of Guzmán's education as a *pícaro* thus takes on the fascinating and often disturbing configuration of repeated digestive crises, as he appears to "peck" for physical sustenance in a hostile world. On an immediately perceptible level that excites little critical reflection, Alemán has his narrator employ in the narrative of many episodes the carnivalesque motifs of bodily functions—eating, sex, and defecation—that form an important subtext for the *Lazarillo* and many of the novel's other sources and continue to become even more prominent in later works of the picaresque genre.[10] But what is striking in the *Guzmán* is the function of digestive metaphors, in particular, in the formulation of the novel's theoretical underpinnings. Cycles of eating and evacuation may give an appearance of realism to the fictive account that we hold, and the gross, material allusions, juxtaposed to Guzmán's sermons, provide comic relief. But the insistent repetition of metaphors of ingestion, digestion, and evacuation also provides a more profound continuity to the narration of the novel. Beginning with I, 1, we find that eating and vomiting, and functions metonymically associated with ingestion—smelling, seeing, touching—serve also to concretize the more abstract process of reception and interpretation that accompanies communication. Despite their apparently antithetical relationship to the conceptual center of the novel, these successive references to the physical serve to explore relationships of meaning and principles of reception that point to a more generalized register of representation.

Instead of focusing directly on the dangerous potential that lies in his mastery of language, the clever narrator simply displaces the readers' attention at the start of the narrative onto other operations of the mouth. The analogic relationship between eating and speaking reveals itself only slowly, as the narrative explores through the examples of diverse pranks the relationship between digestive metaphors and linguistic deception. Readers thus notice the frequency of references to foodstuff and eating long before they begin to reflect on the relationship between the misleading morsels that "Guzmanillo" and other characters swallow, the verbal medium that has defined them incorrectly, and the resulting effects upon their honor. That items of the material economy serve as metaphors for language itself becomes clearer at the middle of the novel, when in his pranks with food—sweets—Guzmán clearly reveals their underlying linguistic support, and the link between his tantalizing language and honor—both his and his patron's—comes to the forefront.

Modern readers have come to recognize the importance of the *Guzmán* and the nascent picaresque genre as indicators of the status of "new men" in Spanish society during the Golden Age. By parodying the supplanting of traditionally inherent "honor" (virtue, blood) in extraliterary reality with the equation of "honor" with social prestige, the character Guzmán seeks from the beginning of the narrative to remedy his deficiencies of birth and fortune, and to obtain responses of favor or respect from those around him by capitalizing on language learned from his parents. To educate readers, throughout Part I the narrator gradually directs their attention to the virtuosity of his *pico* or mouth, and identifies it as his trademark—the source of his self-esteem—through circuitous references to the basic physical function of the mouth and in turn, by analogy, to the larger metaphoric operation of language.

Guzmán's request for his audience's approval from the early pages of the novel on indicates that linguistic "honor" needs a context of communication to exist, and therefore depends on positive reception as well as upon the abilities of the speaker who articulates it. This concept of honor, defined extrinsically, shapes the narrative of Guzmán's life in a number of important ways. First, it establishes his dependency on a social context of destinaries for his communication, for Guzmán derives his esteem only through others' apprehension of his created figure. Second, it leads him to vary strategies of deception and to direct them to recipients from different walks of life as he searches for a public whose response will constitute "honor" and accomplish his social elevation in the most unassailable terms. Third, Guzmán seeks to encode the responses of society to his communication by type-casting others initially according to critical acumen and then quickly through their redefinition as victims of his figural creations. By representing the responses of characters within the narrative to the drives of his communication, the narrator Guzmán clearly intends to inform the competency of readers of his lifestory. This system of shifting perspectives functions paradoxically both to educate Alemán's readers to the dangers of deception and, as will be discussed further in Chapter 3, simultaneously to confuse them about Guzmán's own practice of it. The narrative thereby causes readers to honor Alemán's narrator with a respect that increases as does their mounting suspicion regarding his alleged conversion and repudiation of duplicity. As Ife argues (127), readers are fully intended to experience the deception they read of, so that their critical knowledge of the work's mechanisms will be fully informed: "To be 'desengañado' the reader must first be 'engañado'; he must know the pitfalls by experiencing them in his reading, by experiencing them as *consejas* [entertaining fictions] as well as *consejos* [advice]."

In the narrative, Guzmán's strategy deceives two types of victims, as he experiments with different ways to obtain prestige or fame. The distinction made by Alemán between the general public and the prudent elite among the real readers is mirrored within the novel, as we have already noted in Chapter 1: Guzmán plays *burlas* of stealth on ignorant victims who correspond to the classification of the general public (*vulgo*) in order to acquire material wealth and the temporary prestige or "honor" that it may bring him; and he deceives courtiers—his social superiors, referred to as "discretos" (the "prudent elite")—by openly displaying artifice in performed tricks and verbal jokes in order to win the more lasting response of their favor and admiration. Eoff (*Picaresque Psychology*, 112) observes that "this continuous oscillation between lower and higher social levels marks the general pattern of his entire career," but Alemán's protagonist clearly prefers deceiving the latter. The respect of those who can immortalize Alemán's narrator in court circles is posited as a more tempting goal than Guzmán's victimization of the ignorant in financially remunerative *burlas pesadas* (dangerous or prejudicial practical jokes), for it accomplishes a figurative elevation of rank that sidesteps the uncertainties of recently acquired rank in the material world.

It is Guzmán's search for this special audience of *discretos* that compels him to leave his mother and life in the picaresque subculture of Seville and to head for the center of political power and prestige at Court:

> Hícelo punto de honra. . . . Con esto determiné pasar adelante y por entonces a Madrid; que estaba allí la corte, donde todo florecía, con muchos del Tusón, muchos grandes, muchos titulados, muchos prelados, muchos caballeros, gente principal. . . . Parecióme que por mi persona y talle todos me favorecieran y allá llegado anduvieran a las puñaladas haciendo diligencia sobre quién me llevara consigo. (I, 2, 1: 255)[11]

> [I made it a point of honor. . . . With this I decided to continue onward to Madrid; for the Court was there, where everything flourished, with many of the Golden Fleece, many grandees, many titled noblemen, many prelates, many gentlemen, illustrious people. . . . It seemed to me that everyone would favor me for my person and figure and that once I had arrived there they would fight over who would take me into service.]

As his quest begins to take on the spatial configuration of an extended journey, Guzmán's trials and errors follow suit. He is victimized, and he in return victimizes members of the *vulgo*, or public at large, until his early experience teaches him more about the expertise required for communications with *discretos*, the prudent. In both parts of the novel Guzmán repeatedly robs and swindles members of the former group in order to buy the trappings of a courtier or person of "honor." Such *burlas* secure for him only temporary respectability and material well-being—a limited lateral mobility—but do not permit him to ascend the social ladder. Yet at the midpoint of the novel, after his wiles have been improved by experience and formal schooling, he is able to better his situation by moving from a life of street crime to the households of the nobility. He enters the service of influential courtiers—the presumably "prudent"—as a buffoon, or jester, and receives praise instead for displaying the artistry of his tricks (I, 3 and II, 1).

The narrator Guzmán discloses to the novel's readers these jesting deceptions designed to please social superiors with particular detail and interest. In effect, he thus rises to the level of a literary jester, seeking through narrative representation of experience to win the approval of readers, who may either flatter themselves with the label of "prudent" for their comprehension and applause of his tactics as trickster, or else admit that their distrust of Guzmán's techniques may be tantamount to the incomprehension and stupidity of the general public. The narrative of Guzmán's efforts to deceive sophisticated fictive audiences who control his fate provides a structural blueprint for the literary communication that would-be prudent readers have in hand: in order to trick influential recipients of his *burlas* without angering them, and thus endangering his enterprise, the narrator has developed a special class of *burlas*. He "deceives with the truth," demonstrating visible evidence or "reality" paradoxically to be illusory in nature, so that ultimately his victims cannot condemn his manipulative tactics for having deceived them. His art of deception points to their own faulty perceptions and judgments. In return Guzmán is granted elevated status as his employers' advisor and the master of their wills:

> Por ello y otras cosas anejas a ello me traían vestido, era el regalado, el de la privanza, el familiar, el dueño de mi amo y aun de todos los interesados en ser sus amigos y llegados.
>
> Yo era la puerta principal para entrar en su gracia y el señor de su voluntad. Yo tenía la llave dorada de su secreto: habíame vendido su libertad.... (II, 1, 2: 49)

> [For this and other things related to it they dressed me up. I was the pampered one, the one in favor, the confidant, the owner of my master and moreover of all those desirous of being his friends and inner circle.
>
> I was the main portal to his favor and the lord of his will. I held the golden key to his secret: he had sold me his freedom....]

The unfolding of Guzmán's narrative serves to deconstruct the communications that facilitate his surprising transition from servant to master. To make this process of manipulation or "victimization" clearer, Alemán's narrator is first made to portray it from the victim's perspective, ironically selecting himself as the subject. In a patently self-interested change of perspective, the narrator doffs the metafictive guise of *homo litteratus* and jester to pose temporarily for the reader's or audience's function, causing an attendant and deliberate shift in our view of him, from criminal to unwitting innocent.

Guzmán: From Recipient to Author of Jokes

GUZMAN, THE DUPE

Before Guzmanillo is able to fend for himself and to assure his own "honor" through the artistry of language, he undergoes a process of disillusionment and growing awareness after falling victim to the deception of the world around him. We learn in Part I, Chapter 3 that when he abandoned Seville as a boy, Guzmanillo was prepared to use the *pícaro*'s wiles learned from his parents to elevate himself, without realizing that they formed part of a much larger economy in which others practiced the same art. In the first phase of his wanderings (the rest of Part I, Book 1), Guzmán tells us that he suffered public humiliation as a result of the self-serving intentions and verbal wiles of more experienced *pícaros*. In each episode readers learn through Guzmán to become more astute judges of deceit, while finding that the practice of verbal deception constitutes a widespread social and moral problem. This is illustrated early on in two sequentially narrated scenes in which innkeepers victimize the boy Guzmanillo with offers of inedible food. Joly argues (*La Bourle et son interprétation*, 335 and 487–523) that the series of food frauds staged at inns in Part I, Books 1 and 2 are particularly instructive illustrations of the dual process she designates "burlar" (to trick) and "burlarse" (to be the victim of one's own wiles) (10–11) that characterizes communication in the novel, for they depict the withholding of desired objects ("burlar") and subsequent loss of the same by the agents ("burlarse") when the latter also fall prey to fraud in verbal contexts well-known to Alemán's readers. In these early episodes the author activates the readers' expectations of a larger context of *burlas* with familiar folkloric characters, situations, and lexical registers, while submitting this popular material to a rhetorical process of "defolklorization" that alerts them to the complex social commentary conveyed through the *burlas* themselves.

In Chapter 3 Guzmanillo leaves home dressed as a young man of means. He stops on the road to order a meal from a sly innkeeper, who quickly seizes on his naïvete, perceiving him to be both immature and inexperienced (I, 1, 3: 147). She calls him "bobito" (little fool) and "hijo" (son) with maternal solicitousness, but grossly overcharges him for a meal of dirty bread and an omelet containing chick embryos. Guzmanillo is driven by hunger to suffer her *burla*, even though he is suspicious of the crunching "tiernecitos huesos" (tender little bones) in the egg dish (147–48). Soon after leaving the inn he vomits up the remains on the road and his fears are confirmed by the physical evidence before him. Unfortunately, he has no means of avenging himself. This first culinary example reveals a Guzmán totally subject to the deceptive acts of others. His analytical skills reflect the early phase of his career; as we soon discover, the mature narrator Guzmán will educate the readers to a more complex evaluation of his communication with others by tracing his own learning process in experiential increments that are linked by foodstuff and ingestion.

To reinforce this point, Alemán has Guzmán repeat the incident, elaborating metaphors of ingestion but with a slight difference: previous experience with the innkeeper leads to the character's more cautious analysis of a second innkeeper's behavior. Guzmanillo next meets a muleteer, or "guardian angel," who guides him to a second inn, where another eating scene takes place.[12] Here the future narrator meets with further insults. He is served foul-smelling dishes of mule meat called "veal" by the innkeeper, but trusting his senses this time, he refuses to eat. His suspicions are confirmed the following morning when he discovers the mule's hidden carcass.

Guzmán observes that in this second incident he was led to suspect deception long before he could prove it, merely by paying close attention to the innkeeper's words. Watching Guzmanillo and the muleteer closely, apparently to see if they recognized the illegal meat, the innkeeper had mistaken the muleteer's laughter for discovery of the substitution and rushed to the table in an unjustified defense of the repast: "«¡Voto a tal, que es de ternera, no tiene de qué reírse, cien testigos daré si es necesario!»" ["I swear upon it, that it is of veal, you have no reason to laugh, I'll provide one hundred witnesses if necessary!"] (I, 1, 5: 174). The innkeeper's superimposition of justificatory comments in a context that seems to require no explanation arouses Guzmanillo's suspicions of fraud: "por sólo habello jurado mentía, porque la verdad no hay necesidad que se jure . . ." [he lied simply by having sworn it, since there is no need to swear to evident truth . . .] (5: 178). In effect, the truth soon to manifest itself in the meat itself is brought to prominence by the very oaths that contradict it. Readers receive forewarning from the clever narrator at the beginning of his account that language may well serve to obscure or contradict rather than to clarify, and that its defensive posture almost surely indicates the speaker's guilt.

Guzmanillo's behavior in this episode shows us a more critical response to deception than we have seen in the example of the first *burla*. He does not even test the deception offered him, but rejects it from the outset. The boy's response to deceit in this embryonic narrational sequence foreshadows problems awaiting the readers on a much larger scale in the narration of the novel as a whole, for the innkeeper's verbal offerings of "veal" contain in miniature elements of the "repast" offered by Guzmán's own narrative banquet. After Part I, Book 1, the narrator begins to confess the "truth" of his own life as a trickster, and yet he insists on telling us how the evidence should be judged by explaining it with passages of misleading narration. His own strategy is suspiciously similar to the innkeeper's use of superfluous and contradictory oaths about the meat. In order to respond to Guzmán's verbal "smorgasbord" as true *discretos*, prudent readers presumably must not swallow the deceptions served up in his narration.[13] For the discerning audience, the pleasure of Guzmán's account is to be found at another level, namely, in the structure of its varied *burlas*.

GUZMAN, THE JOKER: "LICENSED" VERSUS "CREATIVE" PETTY THEFT

As he reflects on his past in subsequent books of the novel, Guzmán illustrates further the lessons learned in Book I. A model victim of deception, the boy Guzmanillo soon finds it necessary both to guard against it as listener or recipient and to learn to perfect his own manipulative art. Beginning with Part I, Book 2, the boy learns to secure his needs and to avoid disgrace by countering the wiles of others with the creation of his own fictions.[14] Assuming that we have been persuaded to see him as an innocent victim of circumstances after reading the mishaps of Book 1, the narrator Guzmán then tells us in Book 2 that he was forced to take up the office of a *pícaro* (*picardía*) (I, 2, 2: 263). He ceases to be the victim of food and instead uses it to play self-serving pranks on others.

Depicting himself as a scullery boy, the narrator Guzmán proceeds in Chapters 5 and 6 of Book 2 to describe the hierarchy of deceptions in a palace kitchen under the control of the head cook.[15] Two principal motives of the novel thus develop simultaneously: shifting from inns to palace, the narrative invokes spatial movement to draw the protagonist and reader closer to the work's thematic center—the society of courtiers or the prudent elite crucial to Guzmán's enterprise of finding the proper audience to appreciate his "honorable parts." The narrator also begins to dissect methods of deception attributed to his past, introducing and duplicating within the narrative the densely autocritical perspective of his controlling authorial discourse. From this point on Guzmán has his younger self, Guzmanillo, reflect on types and methods of representation, in a misleading "prefiguration" of the same narrational procedure that directs the entire story.

Briefly, in this next narrative cluster household servants are encouraged by the cook to pilfer leftovers from the kitchen stores and sell them on the street, provided that they share the profits with him. The leftovers, already rotting, are routinely covered with sauces and garnishes to look more appetizing, and hence are easier to sell (I, 2, 5: 298–99). Once again, foodstuff is used to concretize a process of symbolic representation: the overlay of sauces and garnishes allows often indigestible products to be marketed for profit. The mistaking of the figurative for the literal in this section vividly recalls for readers the naive reception that defines the general public.

In the pranks involving foodstuff and its containers in Chapters 5 and 6 of Book 2, Guzmanillo masters and surpasses deceptive narratives worked on him by others in Book 1. Instead of simply lying about these objects of consumption, he traffics in them by deceiving with the truth, a narrative technique that will become increasingly important as he ascends from interactions in a lower social stratum—with the *vulgo*—to communications with influential courtiers—or, presumably, *discretos*.

Readers learn that the system of misrepresentation regulating the kitchen provided a perfect backdrop for Guzmanillo's own self-interested deceptions. He appropriated the techniques of more experienced peers to experiment with his own pilfering and substitutions, while directing suspicion toward those servants who already enjoyed notoriety for similar types of deception. In one class of deceptions found in Chapter 5, Guzmanillo misplaces food in the kitchen in order to facilitate stealing it later in the day. In the event that it is missed, he is able to credit himself by producing what was in truth only misplaced: "Muchas cosas que hurtaba las escondía en la misma pieza donde las hallaba, *con intención que si en mí sospechasen, sacarlas públicamente, ganando crédito* para adelante . . ." [Many things that I stole I hid in the same piece of furniture where I found them, *with the intention that if they suspected me, of removing them in public view, thereby gaining credit* for the future . . .] (I, 2, 5: 291, my emphasis). Even at this early stage of development, one of Guzmanillo's most salient traits is the creation of incorrect assessment of his actions with cover stories to confuse a suspicious audience. Despite the constraints of his apprenticeship to the cook, Guzmanillo creates an underground economy in which the values assigned to food fluctuate according to their linguistic articulation. The mature narrator's public exposure of his behavior as a charitable service to readers imitates suspiciously the structural model of this early narrative pattern, in which the negative value of bait for deception is contradicted by the discourse that serves to explain it. Guzmán's work as a kitchen boy provides simply the first instance of what proves in the novel to be a highly organized series of mediating narrations presented to both fictive and real audiences.

Guzmanillo's most notable *burla* as kitchen boy highlights this strategy. He surpasses the wiles of his master, the cook, when he temporarily appropriates a silver goblet in order to turn a tidy profit without actually stealing it. He takes the goblet to a silversmith and, like an obedient servant, contracts to have it cleaned and polished for the price of two *reales*. Since he has already established his credibility with past discoveries of "lost" items, the cook's wife, who first notices that the goblet is missing, never suspects Guzmanillo. Afraid of her husband's anger, she confides in Guzmanillo himself, who cleverly advises her to purchase a similar one and to tell her husband that the old one is being cleaned. Safe from accusation by either of his masters or the silversmith, Guzmanillo accepts eight *reales* from the wife for the secret purchase of a new goblet, pockets six en route, and picks up the polished goblet for two. He thus manipulates the woman into deceiving her husband with the truth, while removing himself from the scene of the crime (I, 2, 5: 292–94).

This is the first of many instances in which the narrator focuses our attention on his preferred method of deception. As he runs increased risk in the narrative, either because he appropriates things of value or because he harms victims capable of retaliation, we see that the character Guzmanillo learns to incorporate as much truth as possible into his deceit in order to make his culpability more difficult to verify. By erasing perceptible discrepancies between his words and the reality to which they refer, Guzmán places the burden of correct interpretation on his audience. This strategy gives him a distinct advantage in his quest for "honor" or various forms of profit and reward. Audiences who fail to recognize that his words do not depict "reality" literally behave like the general public, swallowing the bait of his *burla*. They are forced to surrender things of material value to Guzmán, enabling him to fulfill one of his major goals. But by the end of Book 2, the developing *pícaro* masters the transition from playing pranks on the less discerning public for material profit to performing witty *burlas* that challenge "the prudent" to detect and reward him for their complexity. As they near the midpoint of the novel, readers thus are forced to reevaluate the *pícaro* Guzmanillo's communications in light of their intellectual sophistication and complexity.

In describing his work as kitchen boy, the narrator distinguishes between "los hurtillos de invención" (creative pilfering) or *burlas* of his own artifice, such as that of the goblet, and "los de permisión" (licensed pilfering), such as food sales, obligatory and to gain favor with the cook (I, 2, 5: 294–95).[16] In the course of Book 2, he rejects the latter, which require servitude and no skill, in favor of those that are creative, inspired by his own genius.[17] Such deceptions allow the young narrator to operate at will, without the permission or the knowledge of his masters and in breach of the implicit contractual relationship that controls his behavior as an inferior. Guzmán discloses that breaking the rules was in fact more tempting to him; he would rather be the cock that "already crowed" than have the profit itself, fulfilling a goal far more important than that of material gain.[18] His inability to restrain himself from undercutting the cook's system of deception with noteworthy "creative pilfering," however, finally causes his dismissal.

Guzmanillo's apprenticeship as a scullery boy is brought to an abrupt end in a grotesque incident with eggs, which gives particular plasticity to his oscillation between misrepresentation that is licensed and creative, independent *burlas*. Increasing success has gone to his head and he is seized by a desire to flaunt his identity as a coverup artist. Wandering about the house in an old shirt and ripped doublet, Guzmanillo originally considers theft of "un par de huevos" (a couple of eggs) from the cook's quarters without payment of the required *quid pro quo*. With his customary cockiness, the boy can not resist stuffing his clothes with more eggs than he can carry or than the torn doublet is able to conceal and he ends up broadcasting the theft:

> Yo estaba cansado de pelar aves, limpiar almendras y piñones, calentar aguas y otras cosas. Andaba con una camisilla vieja y un juboncillo roto. De lo que cupo al cuarto de mi amo había una canasta de huevos; lleguéme por par y echéme entre camisa y carnes unos pocos y otros en las faltriqueras de los calzones. Ved, ya que metí la mano, en lo que vine a empacharme; mas diciendo verdad, no lo hice tanto por el interese, que fue una desventura, cuanto por decir siquiera que le di un beso a la novia y no se dijera que salí virgen o que yendo a la corte no vi al rey. (I, 2, 6: 312–13)

> [I was tired of plucking fowl, cleaning almonds and pine nuts, heating water and other things. I was walking around in an old shirt and torn doublet. Of the share in my master's room, there was a basket of eggs; I came for a couple and between my shirt and skin dropped in a few, and others in the pockets of my breeches. See, since I put my hand in it, what the extent of my overindulgence was; although speaking the truth, I

didn't do it as much out of material interest, for in that sense it was a disaster, as much as to say at the very least that I gave my sweetheart a kiss and that it could not be said that I left a virgin, or that, coming to the Court, I didn't see the King.]

He is caught by the cook, who smashes most of the eggs inside of the culprit's clothing in punishment (I, 2, 6: 312–13).

Guzmanillo's excessive appetite and his refusal to obey the contract of which he was a part exile him from a closed system that in the end only restricted his creative impulses. The narrative reinforces for readers the central point that an ever-shifting, self-parodying code is far more effective for the narrator's double-edged communications than is a stable, socially recognized one. Once verbal relationships become predictable, the "audience," represented in characters such as the cook, enjoys the advantage of being able to anticipate—if not predict—the nature of deceptions before them, and in effect to define the parameters of the communication that they receive from the likes of the *pícaro* Guzmán.

After the kitchen segment, Guzmanillo repeats the oscillation between licensed and creative deceptions, continuing to gravitate always to the latter, because in addition to providing for his material needs they distinguish him from the common *pícaro*. Book 3, Chapter 2 provides another example of his rejection of systematic, codified deception in the narrative of Guzmanillo's work as a beggar. Readers are subjected to a new series of grotesque digestive metaphors, as the narrator tells us how he took up part-time begging in Rome as a convenient source of food. In this sequence he comes into direct conflict with the large confraternity of beggars in Rome, because his behavior is inconsistent with the rules by which they live. Guzmanillo only begs part-time and flagrantly offends the rules, refusing offers of meat when he is satiated, although the ironic reality is that beggars must appear needy at all times, even when glutted (I, 3, 2: 377–78). As an inexperienced freelancer in a much wider world than a kitchen, Guzmanillo threatens the effectiveness of the system used by other beggars in the city. They cannot run the risk of allowing his contradictory behavior to confuse the public upon which they depend, and they insist that he either join their order and accept proper instruction or leave town. The fictions of beggars, it turns out, are maintained by a highly regulated system of "obligaciones" (obligations) and "decoro" (decorum), codified in the written text *Ordenanzas mendicativas* (I, 3, 2: 379–83). As a novice under the tutelage of their "commander-in-chief," "Micer Morcón" (I, 3, 3: 384), Guzmanillo receives instruction to conceal his literal state at all times. To correct his previous error, he must accept and consume offerings of food until he vomits, thereby emptying his stomach in an ironic, graphic display of "la hambre y miseria de los pobres" [the hunger and misery of the poor] (I, 3, 2: 378).

Whereas his vomiting in the omelet episode of Book 1 was emblematic of the process of disclosure of truth for Guzmán as well as for his readers, the act of spewing forth semi-digested food by Book 3 has reversed value, becoming emblematic of deception itself. Mobilizing the audience's expectations regarding behavior of the truly poor and invoking Christian ideals that call for their charitable response, Guzmanillo's act as a false beggar of vomiting is intended to persuade prosperous onlookers of his own miserable state. Here the very act of displaying his personal condition before an audience of social superiors constitutes a deception. The message conveyed, quite literally through his mouth, leads to the audience's misapprehension of the facts and to desired responses of favor in a way that offers suspicious parallels to Guzmán's revelation "later" of sufferings and distasteful aspects of his life, in the narrative of the novel. Readers must consider whether Guzmán's narrative does not emulate precisely the procedure of concealment by disclosure that informed his prosperous communication with alms givers as early as in I, 3, 3, despite his protests to the contrary.

Again, as in the episodes of Guzmanillo the scullery boy, resolution of the conflict between the fixed behavioral code of the beggars and his own shifting principles comes when he extricates himself from the former system, which defines him too narrowly, allowing himself to invent freely before the governor of nearby Gaeta. In this encounter, ignoring the need for verisimilitude, Guzmanillo exaggerates self–induced skin eruptions, attracting the amazed attention of the governor, who skeptically observes the pronounced contrast between Guzmanillo's festering sores and the healthy color of the rest of his body (I, 3, 5: 407). Had he altered his appearance with the imperceptible deceptions practiced by other beggars, Guzmanillo's sores might have convincingly attested to his misery and brought him the material reward of alms. But not content with responses that reinforce his social inferiority, the character pursues the desire to distinguish himself, even at the risk of his own security, demonstrating once again what has been all along the primary motivation for his behavior within the novel: to create through figuration the honor he lacks. In the Gaeta episode, Guzmanillo secures the response of favor that he desires from his public; although he distrusts the boy, the governor admires his wiles and exempts him from punishment on the grounds that he is a juvenile (I, 3, 5: 408). In effect, the audience once again is taken in—duped—and induced to respond favorably through a *burla* predicated not on concealment of the truth, but rather on overt display of the representation that shapes it.

Powerful figures such as the governor represent potentially dangerous victims of Guzmanillo's tricks. As the narrator begins to discuss his contact with members of the upper class in the last book of Part I, we find that their capabilities appear to categorize them as "the prudent": they are portrayed as being both discerning and better prepared to retaliate against *burlas* than are members of the general public. The central narrative segments of I, 3 and II, 1 show that Guzmán's representational art both in the past and the present has been directed primarily toward the end of being honored and favored by this elite; the positive response of courtiers constitutes the highest form of social "honra" to which he may aspire. To achieve this end, we learn that he must entice with deceptions that do not leave his superiors socially humiliated, but instead suspend their critical reaction by causing the effect of *admiratio*.

Rather than avoiding powerful audiences after the Gaeta incident, Guzmanillo persists with his deceptions, next tempting a cardinal with his verbal pleas and his apparent skin disease. In this episode Guzmanillo succeeds in fooling an eminent personage temporarily, only to arouse his interest in how the *burlas* are effected. The boy is taken to live at the palace, where he receives employment as a page. While he dons the clothing of courtly society, he continues to function as a trickster: "Fue mucho salto a paje de pícaro—aunque son en cierta manera correlativos y convertibles, que sólo el hábito los diferencia . . ." [It was a big leap from *pícaro* to page—although in a certain way they are correlative and interchangeable, for clothing alone distinguishes them . . .] (I, 3, 7: 424–25). When he enters the service of the cardinal, Guzmanillo's period of apprenticeship to more experienced *pícaros* and his licensed participation in their closed system of deception come to an end. Dependence upon accomplices and socially circumscribed strategies of deception both limits his profit potential and increases the danger of detection by his audiences, who, regardless of their naïvete, are able to comprehend principles of communication that widespread public usage has standardized. The end of Book 3 marks a new stage in his career, in which he masterminds his own *burlas* and controls them by working alone. He substitutes for the closed system of deception that directs the behavior of lesser *pícaros* a strategy of deception not typical of his profession, and therefore not expected by his audience: Guzmanillo "lies" imperceptibly, with the truth. Rather than concealing physical truth within a context of verbal falsehood, as was standard practice among the trickster stereotypes by whom he was victimized in Book I and with whom he studied in Book II, Guzmanillo works active, material deceptions within frameworks of verbal truth. He then dissects his *burlas*, exposing their technique for his audience with explanations. From this point in the narrative, Guzmanillo concentrates on deceiving primarily the audience whose response is most important to him: he performs for courtiers and the influential—or *discretos*—who are capable of giving him a place at court and honoring his deceptive arts by bestowing on him a fame more attractive than the infamy resulting from his street *burlas*.

Burlas as Art

Guzmán's deceptive communications with important persons are exemplified, in a long central section of the novel, in two parallel roles intended by him to win favor and protection: his function first as *juglar* (jester) and then as *gracioso* (comic) for two courtiers. The strategy of Guzmán's deceptive communications with select audiences who are characters is particularly important, because it anticipates the manner in which he tells his lifestory to those so-called "discretos" who exist beyond the narrative as readers. Analysis of this narrative sequence will lay the groundwork for discussion, in the fourth section of this chapter, of the convergence of Guzmán's various discursive functions—as prudent jester, indiscreet joker, and *homo litteratus*.

Guzmanillo's manifest use of invention to improve the language of *pícaros*, up to the incident with the cardinal, has thus far been shown to be incompatible with the secrecy necessary for most activities of *picardía*. Rather than ensnaring victims with carefully concealed deception, the narrator shows himself gaining fame as the *pícaro* who displayed, even flaunted, the fictions he created. Events of the narrative through most of Part I reveal that in so doing, he rendered his attempts at material profit ineffective. Though while in service to the cardinal he once again is widely publicized as a master of artifice, high visibility does not detract from his effectiveness. In the final chapters of Part I and in sections of Part II, Guzmanillo gains renown as a self-admitted trickster and is rewarded by his audience of fascinated superiors: he is accorded privileged social status among court retainers and becomes the topic of conversation at their gatherings.

At this point in the narrative Guzmanillo's function as a trickster or *pícaro* doubles. Previously we have seen him "pecking" for sustenance by relying on the deceptive abilities of his mouth, or *pico*, as novice beggar or petty thief. Continuing the aviary metaphor that opens Book I with references to his crowing in arrogant self-sufficiency ("ya galleaba" [I already crowed] at I, 1, 2: 142), in Book II the narrator adds that "Mother Need" schooled him to survive hardship by speaking through her inventive discourse: "Ella [necesidad] es maestra de todas las cosas, invencionera sutil, por quien hablan los tordos, picazas, grajos y papgayos" [She is the teacher of all things, a crafty inventor, for whom speak thrushes, magpies, crows, and parrots] (I, 2, 1: 252). Guzmán portrays himself in I, 2 and part of I, 3 preying upon unwitting audiences to appropriate material wealth, with deceptions optimally requiring consistent concealment for success and his own self-protection—even to the point of changed identities and geographic relocation. From near the end of I, 3 through II, however, Guzmán's self-portrait takes the bird metaphor and related metonymic activities of "pecking" further, as he exemplifies his own description of the parrot, the exotic bird whose parody of courtiers excites their admiration and laughter. We read that Guzmanillo's beak was finally filled and that he found material comfort in service of his new masters the courtiers. The reference "Aquése te hizo rico, que te hizo el pico" [He made you wealthy, who made your beak] (II, 1, 1: 37) is further elaborated by a following analogy between jesters, specifically, and the bird of the privileged, the parrot: "Graciosos hay discretos, que dicen sentencias y dan pareceres que no se humillaran sus amos a pedirlos a otros de sus criados, . . . Y estos criados tales, eran los papagayos que deseaba tener Júpiter enjaulados" [There are prudent jesters, who pronounce judgments and give opinions that their masters would not humiliate themselves to ask of their other servants, . . . And these same servants were the parrots that Jupiter wished to have caged] (II, 1, 2: 50). This new role—speaking—focuses attention upon the operation of Guzmán's mouth, or *pico*, of importance for comprehension of his narrative. Rather than remaining a self-effacing medium, the artifice of his communication becomes explicit; Guzmán's audiences are made to fix their attention on shifting codes, as he plays with the medium of language to reveal the arbitrary nature of its referentiality. By building his *burlas* on the polysemia of the very words with which the cardinal seeks to control him, Guzmanillo teaches, subversively, that there is more than one truth. While it pokes fun at authority, however, his message, like that of the bird whose function he emulates, need not be taken seriously.[19] Creative *burlas* in the guise of jester enable Guzmanillo to crow, or "gallear," with impunity.

GUZMAN AS JESTER

The central episodes with the cardinal study the operations of language itself. Using the same words to refer to different things, the *pícaro* and cardinal engage in a battle of wits that threatens to redefine the terms of their relationship. While the cardinal repeatedly insists that Guzmanillo conform his behavior to codes that he, the master, invents, the future narrator shows that by using his master's terms he may yet subvert them, assigning new values within any preestablished code. Try as he may, the cardinal learns that he alone cannot determine the meanings of the communications of which he is a recipient, despite his many advantages in that role. As the verbal agent and then narrator of each exchange, Guzmanillo has the primary option of determining relationships in meaning to which the cardinal must respond.

Readers find in this narrative sequence that his position with the cardinal offers Guzmanillo an opportunity to mend his ways and to begin a better life. The future narrator is repositioned, to dwell both literally and metaphorically above street and kitchen, luxuriating in the company of the elite. Assured a comfortable living and the prestige associated with his master's household, the boy no longer needs his former stratagems as *pícaro* to survive. However, the "honras [of the *pico*] . . . que había profesado" [honors of the beak . . . that I had professed] (I, 3, 7: 425) remain his defining trait. This source of his newfound social prestige is kept well honed through his questionable *burlas* upon other members of the household: ". . . porque no se me secase la vaina, me ocupaba siempre en menundencias, haciendo cuidadosos a mis compañeros" [so that my sheath would not dry up, I always kept myself busy with little things, making my companions wary] (I, 3, 7: 427).

We see repeatedly in this section that the young *pícaro*-page is less interested in material benefit from his pranks than he is in both improving and proving publicly his genius for deception. To entertain his master Guzmanillo plays two types of pranks. He tricks other servants—representatives of the general public—by telling them lies that are subsequently revealed when they are contradicted by physical reality; and he tricks the cardinal and other courtiers—presumably "prudent"—by telling them truths that prod them to reconsider their perceptions and evaluations of the courtly world in which they live.

With his tricks Guzmanillo victimizes the general public, or *vulgo*, simply to humiliate them, establishing his own superiority. But his deceptions of the elite, or *discretos*, entertain and instruct while seeking reward.

The *pícaro*'s pranks on the former group while he works as page are generally examples of *burlas pesadas*, or injurious practical jokes. Their primary victim is the cardinal's secretary, Dómine Nicolao, an upper-level servant and—we notice—low-ranking courtier. Placed in narrative contiguity to the following episodes with the cardinal himself, the account of tricks played on this character questions distinctions made at the outset of the novel between the critical acumen of the *vulgo* and of the socially superior *discretos*. While Dómine Nicolao clearly merits the former epithet for his ignorance and naïvete in trusting the boy after repeated offenses, we soon find the same to be fundamentally true of that higher ranked courtier, their master the cardinal. During the episodes with the secretary, Guzmanillo avenges perceived slights and real wrongs done to him by Nicolao, repaying in kind and gaining the respect of his victim and other servants. In one instance, Guzmanillo gives him the recipe of a supposed repellant for stinging insects, which in fact attracts them, leaving the man's face unrecognizable. He also lines the inside of Nicolao's stockings with an invisible resin that softens with body heat, gluing the stockings to the hairs of his legs. The narrator warns that clever tricks finally led to his complete domination of this victim, when he recounts Dómine Nicolao's words to the cardinal:

> «Monseñor ilustrísimo, Vuestra Ilustrísima Señoría haga en él cuál castigo le pareciere, que yo par dél ni de su sombra quiero llegarme ni me atrevo, que lo tengo por tal, que buscará sabandijas que me coman. Si a mi castigo dejan su pena, yo lo absuelvo y lo quiero por amigo.» (I, 3, 8: 440)

> ["Illustrious Monseigneur, Your Most Illustrious Lordship, do to him whatever punishment seems fitting to you, for neither do I wish to be alongside him nor do I dare come up to him, for I hold him to be such that he will search for bugs to eat me. If you leave his penalty up to my punishment, I absolve him and I want him rather as my friend."]

A second type of prank is reserved for the cardinal and his guests. Before this audience of alleged *discretos*, the boy plays the entertaining *burlas*, or jokes, of a court jester.[20] He caters to their desire for exercises of genius or wit, matching their intelligence with the riddles of his communication and forcing them to be discerning. Guzmanillo also attempts to satisfy the appetite of these powerful figures for "la salsa de murmuración," or the "spice of gossip," by providing suitable targets for their ridicule—the *burlas* that he invents subject both Guzmanillo and other servants to laughter while steering clear of important onlookers. Guzmanillo's behavior toward his superiors indicates that attempts to victimize them could backfire to his disadvantage. He challenges their wits with mind-boggling tricks "in jest," but refrains from causing them explicit embarrassment.

However, we are forced to notice that there is an element of thinly concealed aggression in the jokes upon his employer, as entertaining and ostensibly harmless as they are made to appear. In one of his first *burlas* upon the cardinal, Guzmanillo cannot resist stealing pieces of candied fruit from the cardinal's private stores. The motive for this prank is not simply his usual excessive appetite, but rather the desire to be treated with "honor." Since Guzmanillo's pranks among the pages have brought him the reputation of being untrustworthy, his employer prudently has refused to reward him with the care of his chest of sweets. Guzmán, noting that he perceived this mistrust to be a personal humiliation, tells us that he was seized by a desire for vengeance (I, 3, 7: 429). This urge is manifested when the boy ridicules his employer's authority by showing himself to be an equal possessor of the locked fruits, even without a duplicate key (I: 429).[21] After several successful attacks on the fortified chest, Guzmanillo is caught by accident and ordered by Dominé Nicolao to be whipped. Guzmanillo proudly announces, however, that the public disclosure of his clever deception entertained a group of cardinals gathered with his master to play cards. Although he was punished for it, the *burla* also brought him the more important response of applause and favor:

> Diole tanta gana de reír en verme de aquella manera, que llamó a los que con él jugaban, para que me vieran. Riéronse todos y rogaron por mí, que aquélla se me perdonase por ser la primera y golosina de muchacho. (I, 3, 7: 431)

> [It made him so want to laugh to see me that way, that he summoned those that played with him to come to see me. They all had a good laugh and begged on my behalf that I be pardoned that one, as the first and the craving of a boy.]

Other *burlas* for this audience that deliberately work toward the denouement of self-disclosure bring his ability to question their authority out into the open. The first successful performance with the cardinal's chest of sweets, which proved his genius, sets the stage for two more pranks with candied fruit that serve through their example to analyze the figural nature of the narrator Guzmán's language. By midpoint in the novel, at the end of Part I, readers thus arrive at the first truly appetizing confections of Guzmán's *pico* (mouth)—*tropelías*, or visual deceptions, that pique the audience's curiosity, drawing it into a contest of wits for which it is forewarned. These *burlas*, marking the narrator's intellectual and social coming of age, revolve around candied fruits that paradoxically function as signs of both deception and disclosure of it, as Guzmanillo alters both their containers and contents to deceive his master. The deceptions are consumed voraciously by the cardinal, whose appetite for wit surpasses the *pícaro*'s for sweets. Guzmanillo, inversely, exhibits a newfound self control, opting to savor the sweetness of social success rather than to eat the sweets literally. In these pranks he no longer imitates common trickster figures, such as the innkeepers and beggars, by using misleading signifiers (sauces, feigned illness, euphemistic words) to conceal the truth about physical referents (rotten food, healthy body). He speaks the truth, but what he refers to has been altered or "falsified." Guzmanillo fulfills to the letter the promise made to his master in each challenge, but his communication reveals that the terms defining the *burla*—although they are set by a powerful patron—have no particular authority. The tenor of these apparent conjurer's tricks, in which Guzmanillo appropriates edibles of little worth and returns them, is innocent, almost frivolous, and the cardinal may take pleasure in laughing at his jester's daring. However, the undertones of their communication cause the prelate serious concern, as his reactions ultimately show. The props of Guzmanillo's public *burlas* upon this powerful courtier represent visually the principles of their exchange, but the real locus of his transgression is the disciplinary discourse through which the cardinal attempts to control the *pícaro*'s consumption of sweets that are not his. By mimicking the very words that threaten him with punishment and undermining the "reality" to which they refer, Guzmanillo causes both his audience and the readers to consider that the limits they place on the meaning of his words may in fact lead to their own fate as *burlados*, or "tricked," rather than to control of his discourse. The narrator's description of the *burlas* with sweets raises important questions about how a prudent audience is really to be defined. Prior to this point in the narrative, examples of Guzmán's deceptions have established a distinction between the *vulgo* and *discretos* both in terms of their analytical skills and their socio-economic status: the *vulgo* have been portrayed as ignorant and of lower social status, while the *discretos* have been shown to be intelligent and members of the ruling elite. But we are led to suspect considerable irony in the latter definition as we read of Guzmanillo's pranks with the cardinal and later with a second powerful master. His descriptions reveal that the alleged "prudent" are also subject to his wiles, and are able to analyze them critically only after experience of the communication through which they take place. Because of the elevated social status of the elite, Guzmán of his own choice exempts them from harmful tricks: to obtain his wish to be "honored" through his association with the powerful, Guzmán knows that he must not alienate them by actively victimizing them or causing serious embarrassment. Nevertheless, he demonstrates that he is able to control their responses to his fictions much as he does with victims of the general public. The sequence of *burlas* played out on the courtiers indicates that, in effect, Guzmán allows those who can reward him to become *discretos*. He teaches analytical skills with which to protect themselves from *burlas* and voluntarily limits the scope of the deceptions that he performs for them—in the appropriation of sweets instead of gold—in return for their favorable response. Guzmán encourages readers to equate his social inferiority with a lack of power when we read that he is defined as a man of "honor" only through the response of others in elite audiences. But as we read of his *burlas* with influential audiences we come to see that powerful benefactors in turn are defined as "discretos" only by the trickster's own education of them and by his control of the system through which they must communicate. Their status as privileged audience is the creation of the lowly joker Guzmán.

The first *burla* on the cardinal, the theft of his sweets from a locked trunk, implicitly questioned his master's authority and demonstrated Guzmanillo's demand for recognition. The next two *burlas* involving the master's candied fruits further define the nature of their relationship, by examining the communication through which the *pícaro* seeks to alter it. In these pranks the *pícaro* whets his master's appetite for artifice that threatens not only the security of the latter's sweets but also, potentially, his status as master. The hunger of both characters is shown to increase simultaneously: Guzmanillo's for savoring sweets and notoriety, and his master's for enjoying the ingenuity of the thefts by which the trickster accomplishes his aims. As Guzmanillo boasts of his ability to perform impossible feats, the cardinal accepts the challenge and urges Guzmanillo on in his desire to see more successful tricks. Considering himself to be an informed recipient of the *pícaro*'s communications, the cardinal responds as does the fascinated reader, who suspends his or her reservations about the narrator in order to enjoy the next verbal sleight that the narrative has in store. However, having witnessed the boy's ascendancy over the servants and having been the victim of the chest incident, the cardinal is well aware of Guzmanillo's power by the time the second and third *burlas* with sweets take place. This knowledge prompts his attempts to limit Guzmanillo's power in order to save himself from potential embarrassment, by monitoring the boy's access to sweets and by formulating the rules of their game. While surveillance and threat of discipline are designed to render Guzmanillo's pranks either impossible or ineffective, readers find that they result in the future author's desire to counter difficulty with increased subtlety, as he matches his superior in a duel of wits.

Upon receiving a new shipment of candied fruit in sealed barrels, the cardinal initiates the second *burla* by challenging Guzmanillo with their inaccessibility: unlike the chest, the containers cannot be opened without detection. Moreover, they have been numbered, counted, and stored under guard (I, 3, 8: 438–40). Still confident in his abilities, Guzmanillo indicates that they are not safe from his skill (I: 438). The cardinal in turn dares Guzmanillo to work his wiles within a limited context, requiring that the boy's intent to deceive be truthfully admitted beforehand, and that he accomplish his artful deception within eight days. Guzmanillo is to receive either the reward of a barrel of sweets or punishment. After agreeing to the contract and making the constraints even more difficult for himself by reducing the limit to one day, Guzmanillo serves the cardinal stolen sweets for dessert. His action quickly arouses accusations that he duplicated the fruits in storage with a purchase of his own, and in turn it causes both astonishment and disbelief that his claims of a theft could be true:

> Santiguábase monseñor, maravillado cómo pudiera ser. En cuanto acabó de comer y alzaron la mesa, no hacía otra cosa que santiguarse con toda la mano. Y deseoso de certificarse dello, se levantó y fue a mirarlo por sus ojos. Había puesto ciertas señales. Hallólas fieles, el número cabal, consigo la llave: no sabía cómo fuese. (I, 3, 8: 440)

> [Monseigneur crossed himself, marveling at how it could possibly be. While he finished eating and they cleared the table, he did nothing other than cross himself with his entire hand. And wishing to verify it, he got up and went to look at it with his own eyes. He had placed several markings. He found them intact, the number complete, the key in his possession: he did not know how such a thing could be.]

The markings left by his master to indicate that the barrels were intact remain undisturbed.

Thus, the context of this *burla* fulfills exactly the terms specified by the cardinal: Guzmanillo plays a prank with containers of sweets to which he has been denied physical access. The impossible feat is explained: Guzmanillo's audience and readers learn that the contents of one barrel underwent transformation at the trickster's hands long before it came under the cardinal's surveillance. The rules of discourse, which he allowed his master to think his own creation, were in fact undermined by Guzmanillo from the start. Quickly seizing the opportunity for a prank when the new barrels were brought to the house, Guzmanillo had substituted an identical used barrel saved from a previous shipment, weighted with old rags and dirt. He removed his own prize before the rules were established (I, 3, 8: 440). Guzmán shows that the cardinal allowed himself to be deceived by misjudging the context of signification that established the *burla*. His expectations that Guzmanillo's artifice would reveal itself clearly through a perceptible alteration of one of the containers—or signifiers—was not fulfilled: the barrels looked the same. Guzmanillo's careful work from within the discourse or code authorized by his master blinded the cardinal to the possibility of hidden deception—referents that were not expected. Once again resorting with the barrel to a concrete visual image of the inner and the outer, the narrator reminds us that relationships between signs and what they signify are arbitrary and continually redefined by context. The most disquieting note of the exemplary prank is the narrator's obvious skill and pleasure in appropriating and subverting the discourse of his superiors. Yet both fictive and real readers are reminded that the narrator's power has no extraordinary sources; it resides quite simply in the ambiguity fundamental to language itself. Using his communication in the prank with the barrel as an analogue, Guzmán advises levels of audiences that the language of his autobiography is polysemic, and that the meaning produced by his discourse may be the inverse of what its language suggests.

In this *burla* Guzmanillo circumvents the attempts of his master to laugh at him as a failed trickster, or *burlador burlado*. And he makes the cardinal's attempts to control him look foolish by forcing him to respond to what from the start has been Guzmanillo's own fiction. The cardinal begins to fear Guzmanillo's ability to create not only metaphorical "sweets," but also extended fictions within framing contexts that give them an appearance of truth. He realizes that although the jester's pranks are entertaining, they are far from innocent. In fact the cardinal desires freedom from Guzmanillo's wiles because he fears the extent of their power:

> Y aunque monseñor quedó escandalizado de la sutileza del hurto, admiróse más de mi liberalidad y túvolo en mucho. Temíase de mis malas mañas y, sin duda, entonces, me echara de su casa, si no fuera tan santo varón. (I, 3, 8: 441)
>
> [And although Monseigneur was left scandalized by the subtleness of the theft, he admired my liberality even more and counted it for much. Yet he feared my dangerous wiles and, without doubt, would then have thrown me out of his house, if he was not such a sainted man.]

Guzmanillo's inventive pranks on the cardinal attest to his uniqueness as a trickster. He disregards the conventional mode of deception (licensed) that his audience has been led to expect from tricksters, and refuses to perform in a clearly delineated context of falsehood that they are able to identify and respond to with punishment or ridicule. To assure his own "honor," he appropriates the language of his superiors, using what for them is "truth" to cover his own deceptive operations. In so doing, he challenges socially superior audiences with a subversive strategy they cannot detect or control.

Each deception lays the groundwork for the one to follow. Guzmanillo works a third *burla* with the cardinal's candied fruits that shifts attention from signifier to signified when he alters the contents of a single piece of candied fruit. Upon receipt of a flat of fruits that need further drying, Guzmanillo's master ponders: ". . . qué se haría dellas o dónde se podrían enjugar, que tuviesen salvoconducto de mi persona. Porque, como se hubiesen de poner al sol, corrieran peligro aun dentro de la urna con las cenizas de Julio César" [. . . what he would do with them or where he could dry them, that they might have the safe-conduct of my person. Because, as they had to be placed in the sun, they might run great risk even in the urn with Julius Caesar's ashes] (I, 3, 9: 443). His experience in the previous *burla* leads the cardinal to prohibit Guzmanillo from substituting the container through which the desirable contents are identified, or "signified." Assuming that exposure of its contents to public view will render such a switch impossible, the cardinal orders Guzmanillo himself to be responsible for opening the box and curing the pieces of fruit in the sun. Guzmanillo is to return the sweets to his master "enteras y cabales" (whole and intact) at the end of each day (I: 444). The boy responds in apparent compliance: "«volverlas como están, sin que se les conozca falta ni daño, cosa es fácil»" ["to return them as they are, without any lack or damage being evident, is an easy thing"] (I: 444). But he seems to contradict his agreement to leave the contents of the box intact by noting that, even in complying with the cardinal's rules, he will still enjoy much of the "forbidden fruit": "«Que me pongo a gran peligro, porque conozco de mi habilidad y flaqueza que, cumpliendo con lo que se me manda, forzoso he de gustar mucha parte dello»" ["For I place myself in grave danger, because I know of my ability and weakness that even complying with what is ordered of me, inevitably I must enjoy a large part of it"] (I: 444). Unable to resist the paradox of Guzmanillo's challenge, the cardinal proposes a seemingly impossible task: he gives Guzmanillo permission to eat his fill, as long as the fruits are returned intact, without any perceptible lack (I: 444).[22]

Guzmanillo begins the prank in apparent compliance with the cardinal's rules. He does not switch containers, nor does he substitute other objects for the pieces of fruit. Instead he turns his attention to the mouth-watering contents "signified" by the tempting fruits, stuffing a single piece of fruit with invisible bits of foreign matter. After inverting the box and removing the bottom, he hollows out one piece of fruit from its underside and fills it to maintain its shape with packing paper cut to size so that none of it is visible to the eye (I: 445). That night, upon inspection and assuming that any tampering with the box's contents would be visible either in the number of pieces or in the alteration of the sugary surface, the cardinal is reassured that he has won the challenge—that Guzmanillo resisted temptation in fear of the punishment with which he was threatened. Guzmanillo presents the cardinal with the "fruits of his labors," as it were, which he refuses to eat in the desire to prove his cleverness. The cardinal's reaction is to punish Guzmanillo for breaking the conditions of the contest. Yet as the trickster observes, he adhered strictly to the rules: he did not visibly alter the pieces of fruit nor did he eat any. As he himself explains, he chose to disclose the alteration of his own volition, as an exercise of wit: "aquello hice solamente para la ostentación del ingenio" [I did that prank only to show off my ingenuity] (I, 3, 9: 445).

Guzmanillo's deception once again appears to be based on adherence to a set of predetermined rules for which he ultimately shows his disdain. This trick, however, argues that signifiers take their meaning from the specific contexts of the communications in which they are used; in and of themselves they have no fixed referentiality, nor can they be invoked to stabilize change in the world to which they refer. The truth of this communication lies not in the packaging but in the representation of sweetness that it contains. Readers by this point in the narrative are led to suspect the real irony of his life story: even the represented *difinido* or content that is to assign meaning to his *difinición*, or narrational discourse, is figural. The script of Guzmán's life abounds in signifiers, but the narrator—an inventive and self-inventing "figure"—refuses to confine his identity to a single context by which it may be given meaning. The chronological representation of himself offered by his narrative gives him historical dimension, but as the misleading fruit of his third prank symbolizes in miniature, the work we read serves up a confection that is no more "edible" than its container—the "real" Guzmán is as insubstantial as the fragile casing of fruit that he serves his master, and given the base contents concealed, probably as foul tasting. The example of this third *burla* with sweets is comparable to the episode of the barrel of dirt and rags: in neither case should the contents be literally consumed; both serve to alert the audience to the deception of language in return for applause.

While the elite, or so-called "discretos," save themselves the discomfort and embarrassment in store for the general public, however, their praise of Guzmanillo's wit represents capitulation on a higher level, and as we soon learn, indicates fear of the subordinate whom they cannot control. Guzmán's narrative reveals that the cardinal fears his inventive displays almost as much as does the secretary Nicolao. The cardinal realizes that Guzmanillo's pranks border on being *burlas pesadas* (prejudicial, damaging practical jokes). The response of this fictive prudent viewer to the trickster explains how others—the work's discerning readers—are to react. Fear of becoming the butt of worse jokes leads the cardinal to appease Guzmanillo's appetite for favor by honoring him publicly with special privilege, precisely as the trickster desires:

> Con esto hizo, para mejor disimularlo, del vicio gracia. Y es gran prudencia, cuando el daño puede remediarse, que se remedie, y cuando no, que se disimule. Hízose risa dello, contándolo a cuantos príncipes y señores lo visitaban, en las conversaciones que se ofrecían. (I, 3, 8: 441)

> [With this he made, to better conceal it, of a vice a display of wit. And it is an act of great prudence, when the damage can be remedied, that it be remedied, and when it cannot, that it be dissimulated. He laughed it off, telling it to however many princes and gentlemen visited him, in conversations that came up.]

The cardinal even feeds the boy from his own table, hoping thereby to reinforce the limits of their respective roles—his as master and Guzmanillo's as recipient of his charity:

«Guzmanillo, esto te doy por treguas, en señal de paz; [Rico's ed. (425) has a semicolon here, which makes for a clearer reading] mira que, como el dómine Nicolao, contigo no quiero pendencia, conténtate con este bocado y con que te reconozca vasallaje dándote parias.» (I, 3, 9: 443)

["Guzmán, my boy, this I give you in truce, as a sign of peace; look, since, like Master Nicolao, I also want no quarrel with you, be happy with this morsel and with your servitude being recognized by my paying you tribute."]

Guzmán emphasizes the fact that his artifice enabled him to become more than a page in the cardinal's household. His privileged relationship to his master identified him as a jester: "Destas cosas pasaban por mí muchas. Gustaba dellas y de mí, como de un joglar" [Many things like this happened to me. He took pleasure in them and me, as in a jester] (I, 3, 9: 445). The end of this series of *burlas*, however, indicates Guzmanillo's mistaken overconfidence about the social power derived from his performances at court. When the boy loses heavily to professional card sharpers in a game of trickery outside the realm of his expertise, the cardinal finds safe grounds for reasserting his authority. He dismisses the *pícaro*-page, forcing him onto the streets in search of a new benefactor among the ruling elite.

GUZMAN AS COMIC FOOL

As Part I ends, readers find the character Guzmanillo entering the service of the French ambassador to Rome as his "gracioso" (comic) (I, 3, 10: 455). Although the cardinal and ambassador form part of the same social circle and Guzmanillo remains essentially a court wit, there are crucial differences in his work for the two courtiers.[23] While the boy jester is a pampered retainer of the prelate, who supports him economically regardless of his behavior, as a comic for the diplomat he must tax his brain for entertaining deceptions in order to live. This time, the narrator tells us, Guzmanillo is not provided for as a page of the household; he is paid quite specifically to perform as a professional trickster (I, 3, 10: 455). His pranks are no longer manifestations of inventive wit through which Guzmanillo distinguishes himself from the ranks of fellow employees. They are now requested and engineered by his new master. Guzmanillo's wish to keep his public fame as a jester motivates him to accept his new job with enthusiasm, but he discovers that working for a living as a comic denies him the honor he has sought. In allowing his *burlas* to be taken over by an economy that only fulfills his material needs, Guzmanillo once again subjects himself to the jurisdiction of both his employer and potential victims, as he did before in his licensed thefts under the direction of the cook and in his later experiment with the false beggars.

In effect, Guzmanillo becomes a stock character, the *gracioso*, in short comic representations directed by the French ambassador when he accepts the limitations of the "stage" on which he is made to perform. As a result, he becomes the butt of all the jokes that he plays for the ambassador. Guzmanillo's new master is less prudent than the cardinal, and encourages Guzmanillo to play jokes on others that are harmful to their pride and honor. The ambassador's only requirement is that they not be embarrassing to himself in the process. Guzmanillo now mirrors inversely his previous role as privileged, independent, prudent jester: he performs for the French ambassador as a subservient, indiscreet comic, a *burlador* (joker) figure whose jokes are abusive and deliberately humiliating to the audience, and ultimately lead to his own misery. Guzmanillo's efforts to humiliate a clever unwelcome guest in one scene typify other incidents. When a veteran *pícaro*, claiming to be a principal gentleman in need, angers the ambassador by demanding hospitality, Guzmanillo seeks to embarrass him by ignoring his calls for wine (I, 3, 10: 456). The "gentleman" simply upbraids Guzmanillo, treating him as a lowly servant in full view of the other guests; he helps himself to the wine, forcing Guzmanillo to play the fool (I, 3, 10: 456–57).

Guzmanillo's agreement to play tricks again at the request of the ambassador leads to his being denied the type of recognition that he seeks. He invites infamy instead of a clever reputation, as victims direct their outrage at him rather than at his employer. In the most memorable example of Guzmanillo's work to achieve his master's ends, he employs the strategy of "engañar con la verdad" (deceiving with the truth) to harm members of the audience (II, 1, 3: 74). Guzmanillo embarrasses two prominent persons, a captain and a scholar, turning them against each other by exposing their vanity and hypocrisy. Guzmanillo interprets for guests a whispered exchange that he has with the captain, by claiming that the captain asked him to start an argument with the scholar "picándole algo en el corte de la barba" [needling him a little about the cut of his beard] (II, 1, 3: 76). That is, he claims that he was directed to "pull the scholar's beard"—to insult him—by publicly describing the style of its cut as a symbol of the man's lack of erudition. The guests' uncomfortable laughter bespeaks their unease about the potential seriousness of the joke. But the doctor counters Guzmanillo's version of the captain's challenge with his own insult, asking why, if the former really served Charles V in the expedition of Túnez, he had "no white hair in his entire beard nor black on his head" ("«... ¿cómo no tiene pelo blanco en toda la barba ni alguno negro en la cabeza?»") (II, 1, 3: 77). He points out that while the soldier's hair is white, his beard—symbol of his honor and pride—has evidently been dyed black to make him look younger. After the audience laughs at the scholar's witty counterattack, Guzmanillo is asked to resolve the standoff. He ingeniously completes his task by proclaiming a clever paradox: "«... que ambos han dicho la verdad y ambos mienten por la barba»" ["... that both have spoken the truth and both lie through their beards"] (II, 1, 3: 78).[24]

Guzmanillo's joke fulfills his role as comic but it denies his own objective: he is displaced from the center of attention to serve merely as an interpreter of the witty exchanges of others, and is forced to bear the brunt of the victims' anger. He has satisfied his master's desire for gossip and for the exposure of the private lives of others, but the entourage of sycophants and court parasites at the table is confronted with the potential disclosure of their own hypocrisy. They laugh not in applause but in uneasy fear of being future victims, while wishing to silence the comic. One victim of the *burla* seeks vengeance by attempting to assault Guzmanillo, and although he is physically restrained by the others, he succeeds verbally (II, 1, 4: 80).

The episode of the soldier and the scholar illustrates the most important lesson of Guzmán's experience as a character: when he permits his *burlas* to become part of the material economy that provides for his sustenance, his power is neutralized. The exchange of wiles for wages causes Guzmanillo's artifice to be given a value that is dictated and circumscribed by his employer: with the ambassador he becomes a servile comic who must enact and interpret fictions not of his own creation. Guzmanillo is unable to profit from the audience responses he mobilizes. He is made the butt of jokes by his superior for the latter's malicious pleasure, rather than evoking public laughter at this performance to suit his own design.

The context of his transgressions by permission causes Guzmanillo's deceptions to be defined clearly as examples of aggression that are unacceptable in the communication of cultured society.[25] Guzmanillo's audience is thus urged to limit his power by responding with ridicule or punishment that both dishonors and ostracizes him from their ranks. As he serves the needs of the ambassador with *burlas* such as the one on the soldier and the scholar, the comic Guzmanillo succeeds only in undermining the prestige and favor that he previously achieved in his more prudent entertainment, as jester. Eventually he even loses his source of income when he is dismissed for a particularly serious joke of a prejudicial nature, in which his work as procurer for his master is broadcast and Guzmanillo is dragged through mud and manure, to the humiliation of the ambassador.

Guzmán, the Author of His Life

Guzmanillo's practice of his wiles in pranks that he himself masterminds for the cardinal and those requested by the ambassador appears to provide a lengthy hiatus in a narrative structured around his life of street crimes. These superficially anomalous sections, however, deserve their central position in the narrative and the two books devoted to them, for they motivate Guzmán's transition from a character who is both jester and joker to an author with the same functions, and model a circuit of favor-currying service and its reception that will be crucial to our comprehension of the novel's end. Guzmanillo's positions in the palaces of these two courtiers at midpoint in the novel integrate the techniques learned for requested and more inventive tricks among the general public into a new frame of reference, when experience teaches him that with the elite only more ingenious communications bring profit. Requested and directed performances in service of the French ambassador deny the trickster a position of prestige, whereas his *burlas* for the prelate "de invención," or strictly on his own terms, enable Guzmanillo to manipulate his master's desires and to elicit responses of material reward, special treatment, respect, and even renown. His own inventive deceptions point to the context in which Guzmanillo's deceit cannot be controlled by authorities: when the trickster parodies the discourses through which the elite regulate the existence of others and integrates their terms into codes of his own composition, his language directs even his superiors' perception of reality with the same authority that their words normally enjoy. The bitter realization, after his work for the ambassador, that there is no place of "honor" for him in the material world ruled by others, causes the lowly joker Guzmán to plot an extensive independent *burla* of solely his own engineering—the creation of a literary "reality" that will fulfill his desire for recognition, while hopefully resolving some pressing inconveniences in his material existence. After the episode of the French ambassador, Guzmán recounts his preparation as a mature wit in the areas of learning necessary for him to convert his life into a novel. He first refines his narrative strategy in two memorable swindles and then continues his formal education at the University of Alcalá, where as a student of theology he excells at the remainder of the trivium—rhetoric and logic (II, 3, 4: 378–80). There he plots the use of religious discourse for highly secular purposes: to guarantee an income and, somewhat cryptically, to protect himself from future dangers occasioned by past "casos":

Vime desamparado de todo humano remedio. . . .
No hallé otro mejor que acogerme a sagrado y díjeme: «Yo tengo letras humanas. Quiero valerme dellas, oyendo en Alcalá de Henares, pues la tengo a la puerta, unas pocas de artes y teología. Con esto me graduaré. Que podría ser tener talento para un púlpito, y, siendo de misa y buen predicador, tendré cierta la comida y, a todo faltar, meteréme fraile, donde la hallaré cierta.
Con esto no sólo reparé mi vida, empero la libraré de cualquier peligro en que alguna vez me podría ver por casos pasados. El término de pagar lo que debo viene caminando y la hacienda va huyendo. *Si con esto no lo reparo, podríame ver después apretado y en peligro. Bien veo que no me nace del corazón, ya conozco mi mala inclinación;* mas quien otro medio no tiene y otra cosa no puede, cometer debe a lo que hallare.» (II, 3, 4: 363–64, emphasis added)

[I saw myself forsaken of all human help. . . .
I could find none better than to take sanctuary and said to myself: "I already have an education in humanistic letters. I want to make use of them, auditing at Alcalá de Henares, since I have it at my doorstep, a few courses in the arts and theology. With this I will graduate. For it could be that I have a talent for the pulpit, and, serving for mass and being a good preacher, I will have my sustenance guaranteed and, if all else fails, I will become a friar, where I will find it certain.
With this I not only repaired my life, but I will free it from any danger in which at some point I might see myself for earlier events. The term for paying what I owe is drawing close and my fortune is disappearing. *If with this I do not ward it off, I could see myself afterward in dire straits and danger. I see well that it does not come from my heart; I already recognize my evil inclination;* yet he who has no other means nor is able to do otherwise should make a commitment to what he may find."]

These ponderings at Alcalá, which Guzmán wishes us to "overhear," clearly anticipate his use of preacherly discourse in the novel, with the hint that his ends may well be secular. Immediately following is another carefully planted slip that incorporates Alemán's introductory allusions to the narrator's final state: "«No tengo más que barloventear; esto es, echar la llave a todo, antes que preso me la echen»" ["I have to do no more than come about, that is, to turn the key to everything, before, captive, they throw it away on me"] (II, 3, 4: 364). In a curious shift of register from the previous discussion of letters, the nautical term *barloventear* (come about) foreshadows from four chapters ahead Guzmán's final straits as a galley slave. The studious *pícaro* knows prior to his capture that it behooves him to "take a new tack," which will enable him to close the previous chapter in his life or, in effect, to put it behind him, before they "throw away the key," leaving him to end his days a prisoner.[26]

The context of this reference, of course, is not elaborated by the narrator, and with good reason. As Alemán's introduction and the example of his precursor Lázaro should have forewarned us, Guzmán structures his lifestory shrewdly, assuring that crimes coinciding temporally with his role as author do not receive undue—or ironically, even due—attention. The admission of his current deceptions may be hoped to bring him praise as a moral philosopher or political adviser who submits himself to public censure, and applause for being an astute *pícaro*, but Guzmán, quite rightly, does not want the increasing gravity of his recent crimes to capture our attention. Thus he passes from allusions to ships and locks onto other matters without further ado.

The remainder of Guzmán's narrative (Part II, Book 3), up to his so-called "religious conversion," describes additional deceptions in a manner that is superficial in comparison with his account of previous *burlas*. With a silence that offers striking contrast to his customary, tiresome verbosity, Guzmán both recounts these wrongs more quickly than he has others and neglects to gloss their significance with his usual moralizing digression. As critics, we have tended to read II, 3 just as the narrator designed it—with a more rapid pace and less reflection. Let us not overlook the notable change of tempo at this juncture, however. After devoting approximately one book apiece (I, 3 and II, 1) to the description and analysis of his performances as jester and comic for members of the courtly elite at the center of the novel, and at least one chapter per *burla* and its explanation elsewhere (I, 1–2 and II, 2), halfway into II, 3, Guzmán's narrative begins to fold in on itself with a telescoping effect, precisely as it approaches the end—his present situation as an untrustworthy character who has taken pen in hand. We should recall that this sequencing effect has been used before by none other than the narrator Lázaro to conceal the particulars of a very distasteful "case." The lack of detained authorial self-commentary at this point in the *Guzmán* does not necessarily indicate the relative unimportance of these segments in the scheme of the novel; it seems highly probable that Guzmán's brevity here was intended instead to alert readers to an already familiar pattern of narrative deception.

Since our own critical commentaries have largely overlooked the content of Book 3, 5–7, seeing the increased pace, Ricapito suggests (*"Tiempo contado y tiempo vivido,"* 155), as symbolic of the cumulative effects of the protagonist's sins, a review is in order. In II, 3, 5 and II, 3, 6, Guzmán panders his wife and she deserts him; in the last six pages of II, 3, 6 (422–28), Guzmán then swindles an unwitting widow in a scam involving the purchase of roof tiles, and picks the pocket of a gentleman, tricking him into helping to gather up coins dropped, in the belief that they are Guzmán's. The *pícaro* in the same pages also deceives a well-known preacher as to his honesty and reliability in order to receive recommendation for employment as the administrator of a wealthy woman's estate. Book II, 3, 7 recounts in only one page (433) the embezzlement of the lady, by which Guzmán hoped to accumulate sufficient money for emigration to the New World, and his anticlimactic capture by a male relative (II, 3, 7: 433–34). Despite his bribes, Guzmán informs us, he was sentenced to two hundred lashes and ten years in the galleys, and after the attempt of an armed escape from the prison infirmary, he received a life sentence (II: 443). The narrative takes us from this news—which, as a devastating turn of events, would seem to warrant more bilious digression than it gets on the judicial system and hidden crimes of his judges— directly to an account of his continued swindles, thefts, and other *burlas* while serving time.

Not surprisingly, after previous books and chapters have exhausted our attention with nearly photographic detail and complex if confusing analysis of the episodes described, the schematic rundown of further wrongs in these final chapters brings welcome relief and tempts us to skim. This information, lacking the narrator's usually detailed diegetic explanations, seems less important than those ponderings of his life that precede it. And yet Alemán cannot have selected a clearer way for Guzmán finally to show us what he is really like than to have him describe what he does rather than confuse us with how he speaks. When compared to his previous crimes against the general public, beginning in II, 3, 5, Guzmán's wrongs are increasingly reprehensible in terms both of his morality and civil law.

His ascent as a metaphoric "parrot"—discreet adviser for the privileged—has been paired with metonymic descent in the narrative into criminality. Guzmán has long since given up the harmless pranks and swindles of other *pícaros* and the public at large, recounted in Part I and Part II, 1–2, to traffic in sex (II, 3, 5–6) and rob innocent prominent persons (II, 3, 6–7). It is clear that the narrator merited his civil sentence as a galley slave long before it was served upon him, and it seems equally plausible that he may deserve the hanging with which his fellow conspirators aboard ship recently have been punished.

The remaining two chapters of the novel describe Guzmán's days as a convict, including, among other brief reflections, the three-page interior monologue (II, 3, 8: 461–63), which has been read as proof of his religious conversion. While these lines, to be discussed later, have led Moreno Baez, Parker, Rico, and others to analyze the entire novel in the terms cleverly suggested by this segment of Guzmán's narration (not Alemán's, let us remember), Brancaforte and others have recently pointed to the overwhelming evidence in the narrator's own description of this period in his life that he remained impenitent, and narrated from the perspective of a *pícaro* until the novel's end.[27] Cros ("Prédication carcérale") rightly clarifies that we are dealing in the *Guzmán* with a mixed discourse; religious language and argumentation is in fact used to articulate a convict's civil plea.

I suggest that in the final two chapters, Alemán intended for Guzmán's linguistic acts to speak largely for themselves, and thus substantially reduced his narrator's often misleading explanatory discourses. Only after looking carefully at what the narrator describes himself doing in this section can we place what he says about it in proper context. In his edition, Brancaforte reminds us that Guzmán's avowed penitence does not begin with his sentence. Indeed, as a royal slave he becomes more brazen a transgressor than before. Brancaforte (on II: 442, n. 62) cites Chaves's explanation of this phenomenon, that: "«los que están rematados para galeras . . . tienen por coselete y honra estar rematados, y a voces se publica que 'fulano es esclavo de S. M.,' de donde les nacen atrevimientos extraños, *como si fuese dignidad . . .*»" ["those who are sent for life to the galleys . . . take it as a sign of valor and honor to be sent for life, and it is quite vocally proclaimed that 'so-and-so is the slave of His Majesty,' which causes in them strange darings, *as if it was a dignified state . . .*"] (emphasis added). In proof of such boldness, Guzmán regales readers with the flurry of transgressions that he claims up to the present of our reading have constituted his communications with fellow prisoners and jailers alike. The narrative of Guzmán's recent behavior constitutes more than bravado, however; it is structured informatively on repetition of essentially the same communication three times, with three different audiences—superiors who control Guzmán's fate, beginning with the commissary who transports him to the ship, proceeding up to the boatswain, and then to the captain and his cousin. The exchanges between Guzmán and these masters, whose responses bring the definition of *discretos*, or the prudent elite, into question, should well concern us, for they prefigure Guzmán's implied relationship to two higher addressees: the King, who can free him, and the critical reading public, who may immortalize his literary figure. What then is the basic pattern of the three narrated communications with Guzmán's superiors while he is a slave? The *pícaro* ingratiates himself with each master and capitalizes on circumstances—arranged or fortuitous—that allow him both to discredit other convicts and to "pay off" his superior in various currencies, thereby elevating himself above those whose service is involuntary and assuming control of his master's will. The profit yielded by such communications for Guzmán is mobility: an ascent to the company of powers that be, and the right to move among the other convicts on his own terms. Surprisingly, we find that Guzmán the galley slave is exempted from the toils and hardships required of other slaves until the problematic *corullero* (stowage slave) episode. He guarantees for himself the freedom to redefine his context by being—as he was for the cardinal and French ambassador—a smooth-talking, entertaining wit, and an able supplier of his masters' pleasures.

A discussion of Guzmán's last three duplicitous communications as character is crucial to our assessment of his final and most important communication, as author with readers.[28] In the first relationship, that of Guzmán and the commissary, Guzmán incites the chain gang to steal a number of suckling pigs by encircling them on the road to las Cabezas. He uses his own share, one pig, to ingratiate himself with the commissary who is marching them to the coast, offering to prepare it for him to eat. Correctly identifying the commissary's sensual weakness, Guzmán thus obtains freedom from chains to cook the feast and, incidentally, to rob other wayfarers of two small but heavy packages containing valuable rosaries. He passes these to another slave, Soto, with what would seem to be either prudence (to avoid detection with them himself until back on the road) or a surprising lack of it (Soto has already broadcast his unreliability, informing on Guzmán in prison, and may well keep the goods). The resolution of this episode is highly instructive, for we then learn that, as might have been expected, Soto later denied knowledge of the packages and Guzmán succeeded in motivating the commissary's participation in the reappropriation of the jewels, to Guzmán's benefit as well as his own. While confessing quite readily to his theft of the packages, Guzmán forestalls his own punishment, and authors that of Soto by bribing the commissary with offers of recovered plunder. Not only is he exempted from punishment by his confession; Guzmán assures for himself at least temporary preferential treatment. Guzmán tells the truth about his own actions and those of Soto, but the carefully planned effects of his words reveal him to be as scheming as his predecessor, Lázaro. While Guzmán could have arranged to win the commissary's friendship by transferring the rosaries directly to him, he instead creates the role of accomplice for Soto who, although greedy, is innocent of the theft in question. The torture of Soto's genitals that produces the goods serves to repay the slave in terms that are particularly ugly for his previous "singing" in jail, at the same time that it establishes Guzmán's dominance over both men. The context of this particular series of transgressions (II, 3, 8: 446–51) clearly defines the value of Guzmán's confessions, confirming suspicions that readers have been led to harbor earlier: the *pícaro*'s confessions are carefully composed to assure favor and the freedom that enables him to create the terms of his existence as well as that of others.

Once aboard ship, this sequence is duplicated with another slave and a more powerful master (II, 3, 8: 451–63), as Guzmán's astuteness enables him to distinguish himself quickly and to curry various rewards that result in the redefinition of his status as a slave. The pursuit of greater goals this time leads Guzmán to play dirtier pool, and this sequence is narrated with a series of metaphors and ellipses that evoke the *Lazarillo* all too clearly. Quickly identifying the authority whose favor may make or break his daily existence, Guzmán sets about enslaving the will of his overseer, the boatswain, whom he blasphemously refers to as his chosen "guardian angel." Identifying the same sensual weaknesses in this master that he mobilized in the commissary, Guzmán assiduously ministers first to the physical needs of the boatswain and then to his taste for a good story. While our narrator devotes more narrative to highlighting the latter (retelling two of his anecdotes in II, 3, 8: 455–57), repetition of a more elliptical nature highlights this theme in terms that can only be seen as unfavorable. The account begins with a rundown of his tasks: "Desta manera me fui poco a poco metiendo cuña en su servicio, ganando siempre tierra, procurando pasar a los demás adelante, tanto en servirlo a la mesa, como *armarle la cama*, tenerle aderezada y limpia la ropa, que a pocos días ya ponía los ojos en mí" [In this way I went along little by little being a great help in his service, always gaining ground, striving to overtake the others, equally in serving him at the table, as in *preparing his bed*, having his clothing clean and laid out, so that within a few days he already had his eyes on me] (II: 454–55, my emphasis). This rundown finds clarification in two following references. Guzmán works for his master at night: "Matábale *de noche* la caspa, . . . hacíale aire, quitábale las moxcas con tanta puntualidad, que no había príncipe más bien servido . . ." [*At night* I rid him of dandruff, . . . fanned him, picked flies off of him with such punctuality, that no prince was ever better served . . .] (II: 455); and although he is soon taken to live in the boatswain's quarters in round-the-clock service of his person and freed from a galley slave's normal toils, Guzmán makes a voluntary show of rowing and sleeping occasionally with the convicts to avoid rumors: ". . . por no querer apartarme de allí *ni dar ocasión a murmuración*" [. . . not wishing to separate myself from there *nor to give rise to gossip*] (II: 458, my emphasis). Although it is possible for twentieth-century readers perhaps to assign neutral values to "armarle la cama" (prepare his bed), "de noche" (at night), and "murmuración" (gossip), the text of Lázaro's Tratado 7, as well as similar use of ellipses in Tratado 4, were bound to have been present in the minds of the original public of the *Guzmán*. Guzmán's currying of favor takes an uglier turn in this episode in other ways as well. Once again concealing prohibited items of value—coins sewn into his shirt—Guzmán predetermines a sequence of events that will further his ends. The money, known to his fellow convicts, challenges one to rob him at night, and by confessing his own transgression— their ownership—as well as presenting the lure of material gain, Guzmán incites his master to search, beat, and whip eight rows of slaves, nearly killing many and rubbing salt in their wounds, in order to produce the money that the slave will ply him with (II, 3, 8: 459– 61). Once again, Guzmán confesses one wrong in order to successfully commit another. Clearly impenitent, the convict exhibits his old flair at deceiving with the truth, wishing, ironically, to draw the distinction between his honesty and the other slaves' duplicity that will assure him the bed, food, and company of the powerful aboard ship. Readers should note with some suspicion that in the episodes within Chapter 8 he uses the method previously reserved by him for communication with the elite: deception with the truth, which assures that they will not perceive themselves to be victimized and thus will not retaliate.

Before discussing the brief interior monologue of repentence that we find within the narrative of Guzmán's service for the boatswain, it is important to look at the third relationship in this series of communications with his superiors aboard ship. By Chapter 9, his closing lines, Guzmán's efforts have paid off, for the captain, noticing his diligent care of the boatswain, has requested that the convict serve a close relative who is accompanying him. Guzmán's relocation to the gentleman's quarters marks the pinnacle of his influence during his existence aboard the galley, for he displaces the man's own servants to enjoy the prestige and comforts of—he tells us pointedly—his own sleeping quarters in the storeroom of his new master's cabin, and direct access as a trusted servant to his clothing and jewelry (II, 3, 9: 466). Guzmán attempts to persuade us as to his true loyalty, arguing: "de quien *él y yo* teníamos menos confianza y más recelaba, era de sus criados" [in whom both *he and I* had the least trust and I the most suspicion was one of his servants] (466, emphasis added). Nevertheless, other allusions form a system of elliptical yet clear reference to his ulterior motives. His service to this new master, who obviously has influence with the captain, is ultimately aimed at obtaining Guzmán's complete freedom: ". . . mi cuidado era sólo atender al servicio de mi amo, por serle agradable, pareciéndome que podría ser—por él o por otro, con mi buen servicio—alcanzar algún tiempo libertad" [. . . my care was only to attend to serving my master, to be agreeable to him, it seeming to me that it could be—through him or another, with my fine service—at some point to obtain freedom] (II: 467). In the meantime, with a brazen defiance of the risks involved, the convict does not hesitate to rob the same benefactor who may obtain for him this freedom. Alerting us with brief allusions to his relative physical freedom "me pusieron una sola manilla" (they placed only one manacle on me) and with the term "ágil" (nimble), whose reference to his increased mobility reminds us of his theft while virtually free with the commissary ("Desta manera quedé más ágil para poderle mejor servir" [In this way, I was left more nimble to be able to serve him better] [II: 466]), Guzmán clarifies the nature of his loyalty. In passing references that, not surprisingly, find no moralizing self-criticism, he writes:

> Ellos [sus criados] dormían con el capellán en el escandelar y el caballero en una banca del escandelarete de popa y yo en la despensilla della, donde tenía guardadas *algunas cosas* de regalo y bastimento. Yo me hallaba muy bien; bien que trabajaba mucho. Mas érame de mucho gusto tener a la mano *algunas cosas con que poder hacer amistades a forzados amigos.* (II, 3, 9: 466, emphasis added)

[They (his servants) slept with the chaplain in the main compass room and the gentleman in a berth of the stern compass room, and I in its storeroom, where I had stored *certain things* for pleasure and provision. I found myself doing quite well; so well that I worked hard. For it was a great pleasure to have at hand *certain things with which to form friendships with galley slave companions.*]

Hiding things to be stolen, as he had done while a kitchen boy, in the place where they are normally stored (the supply room that doubles as his sleeping quarters), Guzmán freely dips into the gentleman's supplies to run a small black market among the slaves. A parody of suppressed references to transgression in the *Lazarillo*, "algunas cosas" (certain things) here alerts us to Guzmán's continued transgressions. Either no longer besoiled by physical ministrations of a base nature—at the request of his master—or carefully not discussing possible connections between this material economy and sex, Guzmán apparently helps himself to his new master's physical wealth, laundering it in an equally unsavory and potentially more dangerous underground economy. Shipley's negative assessments of the narrator Lázaro would apply well to the more loquacious Guzmán. We are made to notice that the gentleman whom he now serves receives the ostensible treatment of a "discreto." Far more important than Guzmán's care of the man's personal effects is his entertainment of him with witty anecdotes and tales, and Guzmán's astuteness as a politic adviser, or "parrot": "dejaba mi amo de conversar con sus criados y muy de su espacio parlaba comigo cosas graves de importancia" [my master left off conversing with his servants and spoke with me at his leisure of matters of grave importance] (II: 467). Yet the narrator's references to the liberty he plots and the appropriation of his master's supplies clearly indicate that this supposed "discreto" has no more defenses against Guzmán's wiles than do the *vulgo*, or general public. Guzmán simply "plays" him with a more sophisticated set of *burlas*.

When the resentment produced by Guzmán's power among the convicts causes Soto to frame him with the theft of a small silver plate (II: 470) and then, we must assume, of the hatband decorated with gold (II: 472), the power wielded by the three parties of this third relationship—master (captain-cousin), Guzmán, and slaves—comes into open strife that threatens to redefine Guzmán's fate in ways beyond his control. For once words are of no use to him—he cannot plea bargain by confessing the truth or resort to bribery because he has not authored the damaging prank and has nothing to show for it. Furthermore, any cries of religious repentence would be seen as hypocrisy: "Palabra no repliqué ni la tuve, porque, aunque la dijera del Evangelio, pronunciada por mi boca no le habían de dar más crédito que a Mahoma" [I did not respond with a single word nor did I have one, because, even though I might have spoken it straight from the Gospel, articulated by my mouth, they weren't about to give it any more credit than to Mohammed] (II: 473). Guzmán's lack of control in this deception leads, when his near death fails to produce the stolen goods, to a punishment that is highly appropriate for a base currier of favor such as himself. He is sent to work, while recovering, in the "corulla" (II: 474):

> . . . me quedaba el cargo de . . . hacer estoperoles de las filastras viejas, para los que iban a dar a la banda.
> Que aquésta es la ínfima miseria y mayor bajeza de todas. Pues habiendo de servir con ellos para tan sucio ministerio, los había de besar antes que dárselos en las manos. (II, 3, 9: 476–77)
>
> [. . . the task was left to me of making . . . tow wicks of the old lines, for those who went to hike out over the side (defecate).
> For that is the vilest misery and the greatest baseness of all. Since having to serve with them for such a dirty ministry, I had to kiss them before putting them into their hands.]

When Soto and other slaves plan to mutiny soon thereafter and attempt to draw Guzmán into the plan, our narrator reports with evident hypocrisy that he refrained from participating, "como siempre tuve propósito firme de no hacer cosa infame ni mala por ningún útil que della me pudiese resultar" [since I always had the firm intention to never do a vile or evil thing, for some utility that might result from it] (II: 478). He quickly does the one thing that might yield some benefit. From the depths of the stowage (*corulla*), Guzmán attempts to redefine the terms of his debased existence, sending a message of this new danger to the captain by means of a soldier who has come to relieve himself. "God" is deemed responsible for the violent effects of Guzmán's words as informant: Soto and another leader are drawn and quartered between four galleys, five slaves are hanged, many receive life sentences, and the *moriscos* (converted Moors) lose their noses and ears (II: 479). This betrayal of his own kind once again distinguishes Guzmán from other convicts and has led to talk, still pending, of his pardon and freedom from slavery (II: 479–80).

Many critics have confused Guzmán's assistance of authorities in a civil case with motives of religious penitence. But, as Brancaforte argues eloquently, pointing out the narrator's continued crimes aboard ship during both final chapters of the novel (¿*Conversión o proceso de degradación?*, 67, 89), the interior monologue of Chapter 8 taken to substantiate his recent conversion does not justify their readings. To Brancaforte's analysis I would add that the immediate narrative context in which the monologue is embedded provides no logical motivation for serious or sincere meaning in Guzmán's chosen words. First, it occurs during a period of Chapter 8 when he enjoys considerable favor with the boatswain, is given shore leave, allowed to make money on the side, and to sport a new summer outfit (II, 3, 8: 461). Second, the opening lines of his reflections draw attention to the irony of Guzmán's language, for although he protests that he would die before doing "cosa baja ni fea" [anything vile or ugly], it is his "torpe sensualidad" [indecent sensuality] that has brought him to the height of misery from which he might "con facilidad, alzando el brazo, alcanzar el cielo" [with ease, raising the arm, reach the heavens] (II: 461). Since he has succeeded in winning the good will ("ganarle la gracia") of the demanding boatswain, his lesser or lower-case "señor" (lord), Guzmán reflects that he should have no difficulty in acquiring for himself the greater benefits that his upper-case master, "Dios" (God), dispenses for a less painful price. Fraught with economic metaphors ("precio," "cuenta," "paga," "cornadillo," "acaudalar," "comprar," and "valor" [price, account, payment, small copper coin, to amass a fortune, to buy, and value]), the entire monologue is articulated in what Longhurst (97) has accurately identified as "the language of a business deal." In effect, Guzmán transfers temporal values to the consideration of eternity (II: 462–64). Just as he has succeeded in "comprarle la gracia" [buying forgiveness] (II: 461) aboard ship, he audaciously decides to negotiate the afterlife—"comprar la bienaventuranza" [to buy heavenly bliss]—hoping for a bargain. Guzmán clearly is not unhappy enough with his life under the boatswain to renounce it; the language of his narrative tells us that he simply aims to capitalize on his wrongs, as currency for redemption (II, 3, 8: 461–62). In ironizing the discussion of redemption with a parody of economic discourse, Guzmán's musings on his planned penitence hardly reassure the reader of his sincerity. Just as he has won the favor and subverted the authority of the boatswain and others before him by carefully picking the behavior most desired by his audience, so he considers the appropriate angle for efficacious dealings with God: "Sírvele con un suspiro, con una lágrima, con un dolor de corazón, pesándote de haberle ofendido. Que, dándoselo a él, juntará tu caudal con el suyo y, haciéndolo de infinito *precio*, gozarás de vida eterna" [Serve Him with a sigh, with a tear, with a heart-felt pain, it weighing on you to have offended Him. For by your giving it to him, he will add your wealth to his and, making it infinite in worth, you will enjoy Eternal Life] (II: 462, emphasis added). While Guzmán wishes readers to believe that the ensuing trials and tribulations that he suffers prove the firmness of the penitence that he has just ironized, they clearly point to the opposite, representing poetic justice slated by Alemán for the unrepentant convict who has chosen to boast of his wrongs.[29]

Throughout his narrative Guzmán is made to work *burlas* on audiences who are categorized as either the general public (*vulgo*) or the elite (*discretos*), according to a problematic combination of socio-economic identity and intelligence. His narrative clearly encourages his readers to compare themselves with the *discretos*, who are portrayed as urbane and influential, clever and educated. However, it becomes evident in the narrative of his *burlas* with the cardinal and the ambassador, and later with the gentleman aboard ship, that Guzmán's praise of the elite is colored with irony. The cardinal is not able to understand Guzmanillo's fictions accurately without assistance: he must be forewarned about Guzmán's intent to deceive and know the terms of the *burla* before it occurs, and he requires an even fuller explanation of the mechanisms of the *burla* after it takes place. While the cardinal's lack of perception makes him defenseless against the artifice of others such as Guzmanillo, the ambassador's understanding of deceit forces him to invent pranks that expose his own lack of discretion. And the captain's cousin does not detect Guzmán's independent operations until after, by chance, other victims of the slave's wiles point them out as they falsely frame him for what is poetically true. When the abilities of the elite are considered in light of such evidence, readers of the *pícaro*'s autobiography should indeed be left with the suspicion that by analogy they too are intended to be victims of Guzmán's wiles. If we praise the deceptiveness of his self-conscious narrative for entertaining us while revealing his wrongs, we presumably respond as the privileged because we satisfy Guzmán's desire for favor or "honor." If we simply take notice of the deception and the incompatible viewpoints that go into its creation, only to find him hypocritical, we are, in Guzmán's terms, the ignorant general public.

However, while we are unable to compare Guzmán's words with the phenomenal "reality" available to characters who belong to the novel's internal world, we do possess a narrative reality that functions as a bridge. Guzmán's pranks and other characters' responses to them educate readers to be better judges of the social effects made possible by the deception of language. In order to perceive his confusing account as true *discretos*—critical readers—however, we must look beyond the narrative of Guzmán's past deceptions to also examin the deceptiveness with which he arranges the narration of his autobiography.

3
Guzmán Tells His Story

According to recent theories of autobiography, modern criticism of the *Guzmán* has correctly sought keys to the organization of the novel's composition in the narrational present.[1] Guzmán's literary representation of his past is a project clearly influenced by motives, preoccupations, and a self-image that arise from the life he still lives. Desiring to establish that he merits the freedom to determine the honor of his existence, both figurally (in the writing of Part III) and literally (by living long enough to do so), Guzmán's narrating voice selects and organizes the experiences that constitute the narrative to please and appease readers. Underlying the diachronic illustration of the narrator's life—as in other autobiographies, regardless of their allegedly fictive or authentic status—is a synchronic design that directs the incorporation of history into story.[2]

The temporal distinction made by Benveniste between *histoire* and *discours* (206–11) may serve as a useful formal model for organizing the different perspectives through which the narrator Guzmán's self-portrait coalesces, but only if we consider the functional interdependence of information in both temporal planes. In theorizing on the structure of narrative, Barthes ("Structural Analysis of Narrative," 243) stresses that the "horizontal concatenations of the narrative"—the episodic *burlas* considered earlier—both derive their meaning from and simultaneously develop the meaning of "an implicitly vertical axis"—the figurative strategy of Guzmán's discourse. The resolution of Guzmán's message that readers seek, to borrow the terms of Barthes's analysis, "does not lie 'at the end' of the narrative, but straddles it," in its mode of articulation—in the very language that gives him existence. That is, from the outset, the exemplarity of the *pícaro*'s life is to be found in its composition. While episodes of the narrative desribe his communication, the significance of their focus is recovered through the relationship that Guzmán's alleged "past" bears to his present self-articulation.

In his recent book, Ife argues that Guzmán's narrative of pranks, swindles, and thefts is intended to deceive readers in order to give them an experiential basis for analysis and criticism of the narration. He states: "the cautionary aspect of the story will only succeed if the reader is given the chance to experience what it is he is being cautioned against" (*Readers and Fiction in Golden-Age Spain*, 128). Ife proposes that to accomplish this didactic aim the novel subjects readers to an oppositional process of "engagement" in deceptive examples of Guzmán's past that makes them aware of their critical shortcomings, and "detachment" or awakening of critical distance through his present authorial commentary (127). By locating Guzmán's instruction in the deception of his narrative's language itself, Ife draws attention to the true complexity of the novel's exemplary "agudeza compuesta" (compound wit).[3] I must argue, however, that principal segments of the novel containing narrative and commentary invert the procedure outlined by Ife. In recounting his life, the narrator Guzmán does not so simply use the narrative to deceive and digressive discourse of his narration to clarify. Ingeniously, he deconstructs the deception of language by providing detailed narrative examples of its operation—blow-by-blow accounts that should awaken critical "detachment" in careful readers, while he simultaneously attempts to "engage" them in an analogous process of deception within the authorial commentary that frames his narrative. Exemplifying *agudeza*, Guzmán "deceives with the truth," but with an inventiveness that Ife has not explored.[4]

As I have argued, Guzmán's self-representation as a "figure" in the narrative past is a complex and informative metonymic projection of the metaphoric operations through which his language narrates in the present. Alemán's novel is essentially structured on a dense series of repetitions that transect both narrative planes; *burlas* attributed to the protagonist's past serve the aims of his narration at present, not simply as entertaining negative exemplifications of what the preacherly convict tells readers not to do—that is, deception—but as illustrations of what he in fact does in his own narration—thereby providing disclosure. The analysis of his duplicity that is denied readers by Guzmán's narrational discourse is instead located in the repetition of his language within the episodes he narrates. As Genette explains (*Narrative Discourse*, 166), the diegetic mode of autobiographical narration brings the narrator's presence to the forefront, but paradoxically it obscures information about the figure who speaks; only when the narrator recedes into the background by describing with the mimetic mode the context of which he speaks does the reader receive necessary information about the so-called "reality" in which his voice is grounded:

> ... therefore, we will have to mark the contrast between mimetic and diegetic by a formula such as: *information* + *informer* = C, which implies that the quantity of information and the presence of the informer are in inverse ratio, mimesis being defined by a maximum of information and a minimum of the informer, diegesis by the opposite relationship.[5]

As narrator, Guzmán transgresses the classical distinction between these two modes, oscillating continually between an aggressively commentating authorial presence that confuses our assessment of his behavior and vivid description of experience attributed to his past that examines how he speaks.[6] The *burlas* of Guzmán's narrative, as I have endeavored to show, reveal as much about the process through which the "figure" Guzmán establishes his social identity as do words of the authorial present.

This is evident at several points in the narrative when the protagonist is made to relate cameo narrations of his lifestory that prefigure the larger text of his novel. In I, 2, 7 (327) he invents the terms of his existence—a lineage and homeland far from the streets of Seville—that will persuade another boy to sell him his clothing under suspicious circumstances. And in II, 2, 4 (187) he tells a new acquaintance, Sayavedra, the story of his life by carefully concealing the truth. In the version fabricated for Sayavedra, Guzmán traces his work for the French ambassador to a long-standing friendship that the latter allegedly had with Guzmanillo's own parents, thereby attempting to legitimize his own bid for favor at court. In effect, it is the narrative past, described without confusing diegetic intervention, that best clarifies the difficulty of Guzmán's language. Unfortunately, readers find few examples of such clear self-figuration in the narrative without having to digest confusing commentary. Guzmán's usual procedure is to duplicate the polyvalence of his language in narrated communications with similarly ambiguous assessments in the narration with which he frames them.[7] To ward off the duplicity of his controlling voice, readers must find their own disclosure in the information provided by narrative examples.

This chapter will examine the relationship of both temporal planes in disclosing the mechanisms of Guzmán's narration by studying at close range three well-known examples of the protagonist's linguistic artifice—Guzmán's swindles of the silversmith, the merchant, and his uncle.[8] All three are structured upon figural language whose referentiality is ambiguous, and are framed by discursive commentary wrought with the same linguistic difficulty. In studies that highlight aspects of Guzmán's narrative technique, critics have praised the ingenuity and verbal deception of individual episodes.[9] But as my analysis will argue, the swindles are more than isolated highlights in the trickster's career. Occurring midpoint in both parts of the novel (I, 2, 9–10; II, 2, 5–6, and II, 2, 7–8, respectively), they share a common procedure: the future author uses misleading narration to establish profitable relationships with his audiences. It is my intention to demonstrate that they form a self-reflective progression that "anticipates" Guzmán's deceptive communication in the novel. Guzmán's "present" strategy of narration as author is projected onto the temporal plane of the narrative, in a series of discrete and thus more easily apprehended examples of his medium that serve as analogues for the relating of the novel itself. In each swindle Guzmán composes a narrative to induce his audience to reward him. He proceeds from a deceptive narrative based on falsehood and ambiguity in the swindle of the silversmith to an account wrought from truth, polysemia, and only a minor equivocation in the deception of his relatives, thus offering a model of the narrational technique that assures him greatest creative flexibility and freedom from detection as an author: "engañar con la verdad" (deceiving with the truth). During the narrative of these swindles we find that Guzmán explains each event to other characters with misleading commentary that prevents them from drawing accurate conclusions from the events themselves. His aggressive judgment of prior actions in the narrative past provides a textual doubling of the discursive commentary with which Guzmán surrounds these very episodes. As Reed (*Reader in the Picaresque*, 70) states, "the reader-in-the-text accuses, and Guzmán overwhelms and diverts him with elaborate circumlocutions. Moreover, the reader's responses are prescribed, before he is provided with sufficient information to assess events independently." Through such cameo narratives of his experiments in self-representation, Guzmán teaches real readers to examine closely the relationship between what he chooses to retell and how.

The first of Guzmán's major swindles is preceded by a theft in which the strategy of deceptive narration appears in embryonic form; it thus serves as an instructive prelude to the more complex examples to follow. The theft in which he works in Part I as an "esportillero" (basket-carrier) (I, 2, 7: 319–27) involves young Guzmanillo's disappearance with a grocer's hamper of gold and silver coins. As he walks behind the man, he spies the entryway to a series of connected buildings, through which he ducks out of sight only to emerge several streets away with the stolen hamper. Guzmanillo then goes to hide on the outskirts of the city until the hue and cry die down, before departing the city altogether. The theft provides Guzmanillo with temporary wealth, enabling him to purchase clothing and other trappings of honor and to parade as a nobleman. But he is forced to hide and to change his identity to "don Juan de Guzmán" in order to enjoy his profit. The *pícaro* also leaves himself dangerously open to reprisals by not developing a cover story to explain his actions in case he is apprehended by suspicious witnesses or authorities. However, the agreement between the future narrator and the grocer is established by means of metaphoric equivocation, through which the boy undervalues the worth of the coins he carries, leading the merchant to believe his feigned ignorance of both metals and their commercial value. When the grocer asks him to examine the contents of the load before contracting with him to carry it, Guzmanillo wins his trust and gains access to the coins—a valuable quantity of gold and silver—by asking, "«¿A qué caldero llevamos este *cobre*?»" ["To which coppersmith are we taking this *copper*?"] (323, emphasis added). This verbal exchange is fairly insignificant in terms of the character's development as a master of *burlas*, for linguistic deception facilitates the *pícaro*'s quest for an appearance of honor only in the most precarious fashion, allowing him eventually to purchase clothing at considerable risk of detection. However, it does serve as an important marker of the confidence that his discourse may betray, in communications with those who presume to qualify safely as his superiors, within or without the text of his narrative.

The Silversmith

The first full-fledged swindle occurs in I, 2, 9–10, when Guzmanillo squanders the last of the fortune stolen from the grocer in a company of soldiers at Almagro, under the assumed identity of "don Juan de Guzmán, hijo de un caballero principal de la casa de Toral" [don Juan de Guzmán, son of a prominent gentleman from the house of Toral] (I, 2, 9: 347). Reduced to serving as a *pícaro* once again, he attaches himself to the unit's captain as his personal factotum. To ingratiate himself, Guzmanillo plots the false sale of his master's remaining jewel, an *agnusdei*, in order to turn a quick profit for him. We find that to set up this confidence game, Guzmanillo employs two contradictory narratives linked by the common subtext of the family jewel: he uses the previously invented fiction of his own gentility and lost fortune in order to trick the silversmith into trusting him and buying a jewel that is not Guzmanillo's to sell; the *pícaro* also circulates the account of his lost fortune and real status as servant to regain the jewel from its new owner. Already employing the shifting perspectives of a "watchtower" to refer to his own existence, the proto-narrator confuses the society in which he finds himself as to his true identity, forcing those who view his behavior to depend on mediating narrations rather than their own assessments of the actions and results they witness.

Guzmanillo initiates the swindle by approaching the silversmith and offering to sell the *agnusdei* at a reduced price, thereby baiting his victim's greed. The boy justifies his motive for approaching the silversmith by invoking the personal history that he had invented upon joining the company of soldiers: he claims to be a young nobleman, whose gambling has reduced his fortune to one valuable piece of jewelry, which he must now sell. He insists that the actual exchange of the *agnusdei* for money be concealed from public view to assure his own protection from theft afterward. Not relying on the logic of his narrative alone to insure control of the exchange, Guzmanillo insists that the silversmith verify his words by consulting others. He assumes, correctly, that if the explanatory narrative is corroborated, the silversmith will have no doubt that the motives and conditions of the sale are legitimate, and will thus fall directly into his deception. When the man questions members of the company, Guzmanillo's story is indeed corroborated by soldiers who know him as "don Juan de Guzmán" and have witnessed his loss of a fortune to gambling. Unaware that Guzmanillo's nobility was in itself a narrative fabricated and publicized by the youth in order to explain the source of money stolen previously from the grocer, the silversmith decides to trust these references to Guzmanillo's character and to accept the strange terms with which he dictates the ensuing sale of the jewel.

Once he has accepted Guzmanillo's first narrative as adequate explanation for the sale of the *agnusdei*, the silversmith mistakenly interprets all of the *pícaro*'s actions in terms of its logic. He responds as one of the ignorant general public, forfeiting his use of reason as he overlooks crucial inconsistencies in what Guzmanillo says and does while the exchange takes place. To achieve the secrecy essential to his two-fold plan, Guzmanillo conveys the *agnusdei* to the location of the sale in a pouch whose strings are knotted through his buttonhole. During the transaction the youth, whose hands should be reasonably adroit, feigns an inability to unknot the strings and borrows the silversmith's knife to cut the pouch off below the knot. The silversmith warily demands an explanation for this strange behavior. A weakness in the novice author's plan is revealed: Guzmanillo did not foresee that he might be requested by the victim of the first narrative to explain the material detail so necessary to the second that will allow him to retrieve the jewel. Guzmanillo quickly defines the severed knot in terms that correspond to the narrative that the silversmith knows, by responding that he no longer needs the pouch, since the coins received in payment "habían de ir cosidos en una faja" [were to be sewn in a belt] (I, 2, 10: 359). He does not, however, explain how he intends to safely transport the coins until the sewing is accomplished, in apparent contradiction of his previous demands for secrecy. Although this logical discrepancy should alert him to examine the composition of Guzmanillo's narrative carefully, once the silversmith has the *agnusdei* he reasons no further, departing in satisfaction. The silversmith little suspects that the knot is highly significant as one of two indices of theft in another narrative; he interprets the boy's words reductively to match the univocal intents of his own communication in the transaction. The "prudent" among the readers, however, notice the effects of the silversmith's critical shortcomings when they read the contradictory variant of the first account that follows.

Having slipped the money pouch to an accomplice, who disappears with it, Guzmanillo initiates the second stage of the swindle by reinterpreting his empty hands and the knot for onlookers as the silversmith's theft of his master's jewel. In verification, Guzmanillo substitutes for the fictive first narrative regarding his nobility a more accurate second version: witnesses learn that having squandered considerable wealth, he had become the captain's servant and that he had been entrusted with a jewel, which was now missing. The soldiers to whom he turns for help in retrieving the jewel accept this version as true for the same reasons that convinced the silversmith before: they are able to verify the story independently through the verbal testimony of others, including the captain.

To ensure that the second narrative will hide the correct, literal account that the silversmith is certain to offer in contradiction, Guzmanillo verbally preempts the former's objections about the incident, establishing an aggressive editorial presence very similar to the one that characterizes his work as literary narrator:

> Y porque quien da más voces tiene más justicia y vence las más veces con ellas, yo daba tantas, que no le dejaba hablar y, si hablaba, que no le oyesen, . . . Imploraba con grandes esclamaciones . . . .

No le dejé hacer baza; quise ganar por la mano, acreditando mi mentira.... (I, 2, 10: 359)

[And because he who shouts the loudest gets the most justice and most often conquers by so doing, I vociferated so, that I didn't let him speak and, if he spoke, I made certain that they didn't hear him, ... I implored with great exclamations ....
I didn't let him win the trick; I got the jump on him, giving credit to my lie ....]

Backed with manipulated and ambivalent physical signifiers, the *pícaro*, who pointedly articulates for readers a correlation between excessive verbosity and efficacy in winning positive judgments, provides a narration of the exchange in which his victim's accurate version cannot "fit," or "encajar" (359). His story admits that long before he became a man of letters—in effect, all along—he was cognizant of the power of narration to influence society's perception of reality. His message contains an important indictment of those charged with keeping order, ministers of justice, for their judgments are clearly informed by the same stories that shape the opinions of a supposedly less discerning public. Guzmán admits early on, through the narrative of this exchange, that an aggressive diegetic presence assures confusion of the audience; his tendency as author to surround and intersect mimetic description, which invites the audience's own evaluation, with inappropriate or incorrect assessments of his own is thus firmly established long before he takes pen in hand. That is, readers receive notice that Guzmán's overwhelming diegesis has informed the composition of his lifestory from the very beginning and has had a particular motive—to affect the justice that may be brought to bear upon his acts.

Guzmán's use of narration first to manipulate reality and then to interpret it for his audiences is mirrored in the relation of this episode by the way he, as autobiographer, keeps the versions of others from "fitting" into his controlling narration, for while recounting narrative information that urges readers to analyze his behavior, Guzmán nevertheless attempts to deceive them in the same way as his prior audiences. This is made clear both by what the mature narrator says and does not say about his role in the swindle. First, he couches the story of the *agnusdei* episode for us with a series of misleading editorial interjections. The silversmith is branded a liar and a hypocrite ("platero confeso"), a userer ("gran logrero") and covetous of the property of others ("codicioso de la pieza") (I: 357), and Guzmán implies that in his greed, he might have stolen the *agnusdei* had he been given the opportunity (I: 358). In projecting his own culpability onto the silversmith, Guzmán evidently hopes to portray his swindle as an act of poetic justice. Second, although the narrative itself has made it clear that the swindle was premeditated, and carefully planned and executed solely through his agency, the adult narrator—normally given to verbose moralizing—refrains from offering any commentary upon the morality of his own actions. Presumably, while he accepts physical responsibility for the swindle, Guzmán relies upon his immaturity in the episode narrated to constitute grounds for not accepting any moral or ethical guilt. Sanctimonious commentary, which in this case will not serve his needs, is suppressed.

The Milanese Merchant

The second swindle takes place in Part II, when Guzmán as a young man leaves the service of the French ambassador. The narrator tells us that he agreed to mastermind the swindle of a Milanese merchant at the request of Sayavedra, his own companion, and the merchant's accountant, Aguilera. Because the merchant is wary of theft, Aguilera's tantalizing spatial proximity to the money permits only imagined opportunities to appropriate it. We learn that the merchant handles the cash transactions himself, while the accountant's only contact with the wealth before him is through his entries in the shop ledgers (II, 2, 5: 213–14). In this episode, readers find Guzmán quickly capitalizing upon the ability of language to define physical reality. He realizes that Aguilera's control of the ledger books may provide an access to their victim's wealth, for words alone guarantee ownership of the coffers' contents. In this confidence game, Guzmán designs a theft that is far less detectable than that of the previous swindle, for it involves manipulation of signs only and not their physical referents. Guzmán focuses his creative energies on the records rather than the cash, minting a verbal currency by secretly falsifying the ledgers and constructing a narrative to explain the merchant's possession of his money. Guzmán's plan is to have this linguistic fortune entrusted to the merchant revert to him as literal cash.

To establish his *persona* and his exchange of words for money, Guzmán makes two visits to the shop. During the first he lists the credentials by which his request is to be interpreted and deemed plausible: he is a foreign noble who has come to Milan to purchase wedding gifts for his bride. He asks to deposit the money with the merchant for temporary safekeeping. The merchant's quick assent indicates his own thoughts of theft, and Guzmán with equal guile only verbally entrusts his money to him (II, 2, 5: 216–17). Guzmán is expected to return later with the cash that has just been metaphorically "transacted."

Before returning the following week, Guzmán "verifies" the deposit of money to make his case stronger, secretly entering written notations in a ledger brought by the accountant. He also places labels of his ownership in several coffers brought by Aguilera. After he has "legalized" the coins, which he never deposited, Guzmán then enters a written reference to withdrawal of the same coins. In so doing, he makes it appear that the merchant falsified his own records in order to keep money not belonging to him. To insure results, Guzmán mentions in the ledger entry ten coins of a denomination that the merchant does not possess—"diez doblones de a diez" [ten doubloons or "pieces" of (the weight or designation) ten] (II, 2, 6: 220).[10] He has Aguilera secretly add ten such coins to the coffer, assured that when he describes them for witnesses, his victim will swear publicly (and in fact truthfully) that he has none. Guzmán knows that authorities will grant his request for a formal investigation because as a merchant the man has a dubious reputation. According to the *pícaro*'s plan, officials will discover the coins that the merchant denied having, and ensuing testimony will confirm the merchant to be at fault in the linguistically controlled "exchange."

To initiate the final phase of the swindle, Guzmán returns to the shop and makes an ambiguous request before witnesses in a polysemic phrase that San Miguel (217) argues is the most important communication in the episode, for it may signify either that Guzmán's boy will drop off the money as previously agreed or that he will come to pick up a previously deposited sum. It represents the juncture of two divergent narratives that Guzmán has designed for his separate audiences. The merchant and other characters, and readers are confronted with both the story of Guzmán's intended deposit as told to the merchant, and the story of his intended withdrawal as told to various witnesses. Guzmán's ambiguous words fit both versions as he permits each audience to interpret them in different ways.

He offers the first story to the merchant when he repeats his previous statement: "«Aqueste criado vendrá por la mañana con un talego y un papel mío. Mande V. Md. que se le dé todo buen despacho»" ["This servant will come in the morning with a bag and a paper of mine. Please order that he be given quick service"] (II, 2, 6: 220). The merchant interprets it correctly, in the context of

Guzmán's previous communication with him, as a reference to Guzmán's intended deposit of money. That is, Guzmán will send a bag ("talego") full of money together with a slip of paper ("papel"), requesting deposit. Using a reflexive passive verb ("se . . . dé"), he requests that the servant "be given" quick service: "«Mande V. Md. que se le dé todo buen despacho.»" Agreeing to these terms, the merchant still anticipates the return of Guzmán's servant with the money.

To begin the second, contradictory variant, Guzmán demands in apparent afterthought the "money," which he has never deposited with the merchant: "«Después que de aquí salí, se me ha ofrecido a el pensamineto que importa llevar luego ese dinero para cierto efeto. *Mándelo dar* Vuestra Merced»" ["After I left here, the thought occurred to me that it is important to take the money at once, for a certain purpose. Sir, order that it be handed over"] (II, 2, 6: 220, emphasis added). (Rico's edition, II, 2, 6: 659, includes the indirect object pronoun "me," thus clarifying: "—Mándemelo dar," [order that it be given to me].) Speaking the truth and denying receipt of any money from Guzmán, the Milanese merchant finds himself having to engage in another narrative, in which the terms of their previous verbal exchange have suddenly changed meaning. He is caught off guard as Guzmán clarifies the ambiguity of his own request for a cash withdrawal: the "papel" and "talego" were intended to refer, respectively, to the written request and the empty sack for transporting his money (II: 221). More important, however, is Guzmán's sudden revision of his first communication. He repeats the request, together with the merchant's verbal agreement, for the benefit of witnesses, with a crucial yet almost imperceptible linguistic modification, arguing: "«Pues acaba en este momento de confesarme delante de todos estos caballeros, cuando le dije que vendría manaña mi criado por ellos, que se *los* daría. ¿Y agora que vuelvo yo, me los niega en un momento?»" ["Well, he just this moment admitted to me before all these gentlemen, when I told him that my servant would come tomorrow for them, that he would give *them* to him. And now that I return myself, is he going to refuse me them at this time?"] (II, 2, 6: 221, emphasis added). Guzmán now tells bystanders that the merchant promised to turn over the literal coins to his servant: the direct object "buen despacho" (quick service) of his first version, previously paired with "le" (either an indirect object for the servant or, as Lapesa (405–6) explains, a repetition of the direct object itself), is replaced by "los," a reference to "los doblones."

Guzmán incisively establishes the authority of this second version, quite ironically, by pointing out elements of his opponent's account that do not fit the new truth that he himself has established, in a series of allegations that begins with:

«¿Qué mayor verdad mía o qué mayor indicio de su malicia puede haber que decir poco ha que no le había dado blanca y hallarlo aquí escrito, aunque testado? ¿Si lo recibió, por qué lo niega? ¿Y si no lo recibió, cómo está escrito aquí?» (II, 2, 6: 224)

["What greater truth of mine or what greater sign of his malice can there be than to say, just a few minutes ago, that I hadn't given him even a copper and to find it here written, even attested? If he received it, why does he deny it? And if he didn't receive it, how can it be written here?"]

In the narrative, Guzmán first seeks to legitimize the account that he himself offers by invoking learned discourse, to simultaneously indicate his superior reasoning—and implicitly, education and social rank—and to point out the apparent lack of logic in his victim's alleged "story." The clever strategist then escalates his offensive, citing a discourse of much greater authority. He culminates the attack with a menacing flourish of "proof" by presuming to speak for the one judge whose judgment is both incorruptible and irrefutable: "«¿Cómo son vuestros . . . si acabáis de confesar que no teníades doblones de a diez? Que Dios ha permitido que se os olvidase de haberlos recibido, para que yo no perdiese mi hacienda»" ["How can they be yours . . . if you just confessed that you had no doubloons of ten? God has let you forget that you received them so that I wouldn't lose my fortune"] (II: 225). As a young man, Guzmán thus is shown to recognize the powerful potential of religious discourse even before he pursues the education that legitimizes his use of it. The effectiveness of his work as mouthpiece for "God" in this scam in fact anticipates the *pícaro*'s decision in II, 3, 4 to become ordained in order to assure himself an easy income and, more importantly, the appearance of virtue that the discourse of the profession confers. Appropriating a verbal register of greater authority than that of civil law, Guzmán evidently seeks in the Milanese swindle to place himself beyond reproach, and he succeeds. Mastery in Part II, Book 3 of the "artes"—rhetoric and logic—that accompany study of theology will only confirm his ability to speak for his judges, while improving the formal sophistication with which he composes his utterances.

The damaging effects of the words with which Guzmán anticipates his preacherly function are made quite clear in the narrative of the

Milanese caper. The innocent merchant, forced to respond to Guzmán's indignant allegations, confirms the truth of Guzmán's initial visit, unwittingly giving credence to the story of a verbal contract. He also truthfully denies receipt of the money described by Guzmán or knowledge of any written evidence to the contrary. However, inconsistencies in the merchant's response to Guzmán's story lead to an official investigation and discovery of the coins that were supposed to have been withdrawn, the labels "don Juan de Osorio," and the particular denominations of the "diez doblones de a diez" that substantiate Guzmán's story. Guzmán's victim has told the factual truth, but not the truth established by the budding narrator. As a result of gross injustice that Guzmán attributes to Divine authority, it is the merchant who is charged with being a swindler. According to plan, the money legally reverts to Guzmán, the putative owner whose word, quite ironically, has been proven true by the "señas . . . verdaderas y ciertas"—written oaths—designed by him to substantiate his own story (II, 2, 6: 223).

Just as readers are on the verge of formulating some rather harsh opinions about the activities to which the narrator has previously dedicated his gift of gab, and rethinking their perceptions of his character at present, their experience of narrational deception is intensified. Guzmán frames the account of this swindle with deceptive narration in the present, through a series of diegetic disclaimers of his own blameworthiness in which he transfers culpability to the merchant and confuses the readers' perceptions of their respective roles in the narrated transaction.[11] He first relates at length Aguilera's supposedly objective opinion that the victim was already deemed a thief by the public (II, 2, 5: 214-15). Guzmán then adds his own allegations to reinforce claims of the merchant's prior misdeeds: ". . . agora sospecho que no fueron sus pensamientos otros que los míos: el de quedarse con ellos y yo de robárselos" [I now suspect that his thoughts were no different than mine: he to remain with the coins and I to rob him of them] (II: 216); "conformidad teníamos ambos en engañar" [we both were in agreement regarding the intent to deceive] (II: 220). Although he admits to at least equal guilt in comparing their intentions, readers note that the narrator Guzmán devotes no moral discourse to the condemnation of his own role in actually carrying out the plan of deception.[12] In terms of his argument, as Aguilera has suggested, public ruin of the man is intended to constitute, at least in the minds of readers, a civic service to the republic that the man's habitual frauds have cost dearly (II: 215).

If we compare the narration with which Guzmán encloses the description of the past event to the words attributed to both men within the narrative of the swindle itself, however, there is an obvious disjunction. In the description of the agreement we see that the merchant consistently told the truth and desired that it be demonstrated. The merchant thinks that he has lost his sanity as a result of Guzmán's lies (II, 2, 6: 226–27) and is left "muriéndose del enojo, loco de imaginar cómo pudo ser aquello y aun le pasó por la imaginación, no ser otra cosa que obra del demonio" [dying of rage, crazy from imagining how that could be, and it even passed through his mind that it was none other than the work of the devil] (II: 228). Unable to figure out how the deception was worked, Guzmán's victim is finally forced to rationalize the entire incident as the work of the devil. However, looking beyond the mature narrator's diegetic attacks on his victim's morality, we should recall that during the incident Guzmán created an ironic, if not heretical, religious metaphor for his own diabolical manipulations of the circumstances, referring to them as the work of "God" (II, 2, 6: 225, 226). Despite his present comments about the merchant's faults, Guzmán's authorship of the damaging joke is made indisputably clear by the narrative. Once again, we find a detailed example of mimetic disclosure accompanied by intended deception in the narrator's moralizing discourse, as he targets his victim for criticism.

Guzmán's Relatives

Immediately following the episode in Milan, the emerging author's genius culminates in a third narrational swindle (II, 2, 7), as Guzmán travels to Genoa to avenge himself for a night of mistreatment when he had called years before, as an immigrant dressed in rags, on a suspicious paternal uncle. On that occasion the Genoese userer had ordered Guzmanillo to be tossed in a blanket by four pranksters dressed as devils, an experience that caused the boy to besoil himself in fright before fleeing (I, 3, 7: 372). This third swindle is Guzmán's most sophisticated, for in it, with the exception of one minor equivocation, he tells the truth, eliminating discrepancies between his communication and reality that may lead to detection and capture. Although it might alert the Genoese relatives to his motives for a second visit, Guzmán boldly reveals his identity. He truthfully describes his father's life to allay their fears that he may be an imposter. The trickster even admits to having passed through

Genoa some years before, using "como" (approximately, about) to imply a poor memory and an equivocation of nearly four years in the date: "... le dije que habría como tres años, poco menos, que había por allí pasado, sin poder ni quererme detener más de a hacer noche, a causa de la mucha diligencia con que a Roma caminaba..." [... I told him that it was probably about three years, a little less, that I had passed through there without being able to or wishing to stop longer than to pass the night, on account of the speed with which I was traveling to Rome ...] (II, 2, 7: 247). Their gaze fixed upon the young man's obvious wealth, spoils from the Milanese caper, Guzmán's uncle and the rest of the clan do not pause to consider the possibility of deliberate obfuscation in his otherwise accurate account. As Guzmán has previously learned with the silversmith and the merchant, self-interest will lead most audiences to misinterpret truth and falsehood indiscriminately. His prior victims have comprehended the polysemia of his language according to the univocal register most compatible with the reality they desire, overlooking the possibility that he has assigned alternate meanings to the same words in the context of their dealings. Identifying the same interpretive weaknesses in his Genoese relatives, Guzmán points the way through which they will become authors of their own financial ruin by speaking the truth in contexts that are ambiguous and allowing them to interpret his communications as they will. His deceptions this time revolve around the way in which he presents the contents of two trunks and a gold chain.

Guzmán verifies the literal existence of his wealth by gambling and spending it. He then enlists Sayavedra's aid to duplicate two trunks containing his real riches, which are to be hidden aboard the escape ship, with two more trunks full of rocks. He asks to place "two trunks" in his uncle's house for safekeeping, truthfully referring to the actual contents of both sets of trunks: "... truje a plática lo mucho que temía salir de casa de noche, porque tenía en el aposento mis baúles, en especial dos dellos con plata, joyas de algún valor y dineros y, por decir verdad, mi pobreza toda" [... I mentioned how much I feared leaving the house at night, because I had in the room my trunks, especially two of them with silver, jewelry of some value, and money, and, to tell the truth, my entire miserable worth] (II, 2, 8: 261). Left to reconcile what would be a logical contradiction between "silver," "jewelry of value," and "money" on the one hand, and "my entire miserable worth" (literally, "my entire poverty") on the other, the uncle interprets the latter expression as a figurative reference, as Guzmán's ironic understatement of a sizable fortune. Sayavedra then delivers the rock-laden trunks with a statement that is humorously denotative: "«Señor, aunque lo que tiene mi señor dentro es de consideración, lo que vale más de todo es pedrería . . .»" ["Sir, although what my master has inside is of importance, that of greatest value is the stones . . ."] (II, 2, 8: 264). Since he has seen Guzmán's literal wealth, the uncle concludes that the contents of the trunks so worthy of consideration must be precious jewels, pejoratively designated by the figurative reference to "stones." By placing referents of opposite value in contiguity, the trickster this time has transferred the role normally reserved for himself to his victim, along with, presumably, its moral responsibilities. The creator of this episode's figurative reality, as well as of its damaging effects, is not Guzmán but the unwitting recipient of his communication. Ironically, in terms of their yield at the end of the deal, the literal rocks that the uncle takes to be jewels indeed function as gems in the rough. The Genoese themselves, through their interpretation and resulting actions, supply the elaboration that translates the rocks into figurative equivalents of real gems, for they then ply Guzmán with wedding gifts that are commensurate in value with precious stones in order to bring him and his fortune into the family.

During this episode Guzmán also shows his uncle a real gold chain, which he sends to a smith for a written estimate of its value. Guzmán then asks his uncle to accept the chain as collateral for a temporary gambling loan. In another act of substitution, Guzmán leaves with his uncle an identical chain of "oro de jeringas" (filled gold) (II, 2, 8: 270). Prior to this episode, Guzmán himself had been fooled by the artifice of the modest gold chain. Marveling at its apparent perfection, he tells us, he had paid over six-hundred *escudos* to duplicate it in "oro fino" (pure gold) (II, 2, 6: 229–30). Ironically, we find that like the trunks of rocks, the original chain that contains less gold proves to be of even greater value than its duplicate, for it causes Guzmán's Genoese relatives to shower him with groom's gifts that far exceed the value of the real chain.

In this confidence game, Guzmán does not lie about what is signified by his words. He cleverly creates associative contexts in which the relationship between what he says and what he means is influenced both by the audience's familiarity with a standard mercantile discourse and by their recollection of his previous statements and their alleged material referents. The huge trunks of "stones" and lustrous chain of "gold" derive much of their perceived value through synecdochic association with the stolen, literal jewels and coins which Guzmán has used to signify a fictive wealth and social status. Typical of the general public and his other victims, Guzmán's relatives are captivated by the sumptuous signifiers of wealth readily visible to them, and are blinded to the devalued state of his referents. True to plan, Guzmán's relatives perceive no difference between the artful chests of "stones" and "gold" chain and his verified wealth. They supply the figurative interpretation of "poverty" and "stones" necessary to the story they wish to hear. Ironically, they become responsible for the unhappy outcome of this fiction when they proceed with plans for the wedding. Hoping to kill two birds with one stone, marrying off a dishonored daughter and reaping the profit of Guzmán's fortune, Guzmán's relatives warmly welcome him to their fold with prenuptial festivities, without questioning his motives in the disadvantageous match (II, 2, 8: 262). Shortly before the wedding date, secretly set by Guzmán to coincide with the ship's departure, they send him valuable groom's gifts, assuming that this initial outlay will revert back to them once he has married into their ranks. However, Guzmán gathers up his profits from this one-sided exchange on the eve of the wedding and escapes aboard his friend's galley. He leaves the Genoese relatives with the results of what is ultimately their own willful creation of a fiction.

Like the other swindles, this one is incorporated into the main narrative in a way that confuses its meaning and has serious implications for the narrator's reliability. In the pages preceding the Genoese swindle, Guzmán regales readers with a confusing digression—a critique of hypocrites whose "honor" is patently illusive. He moves from a general to a specific focus that vacillates between his own wrongs and those of others (II, 2, 7: 235–36), ending with the condemnation of velveteen-clad thieves whose crimes far outweigh those of "pobres pecadores como yo" [poor sinners like me] (II, 2, 7: 237).[13] The preliminary diegetic bracketing of the narrated incident thus sets the stage for Guzmán's readers, who are prepared to evaluate the wrongs of his social superiors as more serious than his own and receive no instruction to read the Genoese episode with a critical concentration on Guzmán's work as a thief.

We are further discouraged from censuring Guzmán's behavior in the swindle through a series of intercalated comments made by the mature narrator about the wrongs of his relatives. Guzmán interjects into the story of this subsequent encounter with them several graphic and exaggerated descriptions of his previous injuries at the hands of the Genoese. When he hears his uncle's version of the incident with a street urchin—Guzmanillo himself—years before, the narrator tells us:

Refirióme lo pasado con grande solemnidad, la traza que tuvo, cómo no le quiso dar de cenar y sobre todas estas desdichas lo mantearon. Yo pobre, como fui quien lo había padecido, pareció que de nuevo me volvieron a ello. Abriéronseme las carnes, como el muerto de herida, que brota sangre fresca por ella si el matador se pone presente. (II, 2, 7: 247)

[He told me of the past occurrence with great solemnity, the plan that he had, how he refused to provide him a dinner and, in addition to all these disgraces, that they blanket-tossed him. I, poor man, since I was he who had suffered it, it seemed that they made me relive it. My flesh opened, like one dead of a wound that breaks out bleeding freshly if the killer appears.]

In effect, Guzmán solicits his readers' sympathy, grotesquely hyperbolizing the injury done primarily to his pride years ago with material images that evoke Christ-like sufferings. We are intended to forget the episode as it was described earlier in his own narrative, and encouraged to overlook the change in context and reversal of roles that follows in the retaliatory swindle of his uncle.

In addition to the initial moralizing discourse and Guzmán's use of misleading narrative flashbacks, the narrative of Guzmán's Genoese swindle is further segmented by a brief digression *in medias res* on vengeance (II, 2, 8: 252) and a tercet of secondary narratives that appear intended to illustrate and reinforce the critical view of vengeance taken by the moralizing narrator. Like other authorial intrusions, however, this series of comments in fact works to confuse readers. As Cortázar points out ("La estructura de *Guzmán de Alfarache*," 93–94), Guzmán's initial digression condemns vengeance as an act of cowardice that is immoral and dishonorable. But the narrator then chooses to illustrate his point in a contradictory manner by following it with two secondary narratives in which vengeance is shown to be a prudent, warranted response to deception's injury of honor (II, 2, 8: 252–56). In the first anecdote, a widow is tricked by a suitor, who creates the public impression that they are having sexual relations. Guzmán praises her vengeance, which consists of marrying the suitor, slitting his throat, and retiring to a convent, as an exemplary means of saving her honor (II, 2, 8: 254). Next we read the brief story of a madman, who with reason kills a dog that had attacked him (II, 2, 8: 255). A third interpolated anecdote shifts focus to tell of a subject who forgave his brother's murderer, concluding that such behavior was so anomalous to the human condition as to constitute a miracle (II, 2, 8: 256–57). Having shown vengeance to be the natural and fair response to injuries involving honor, Guzmán guides us back into the narrative of his own vengeance for previous mistreatment with a focus on justice rather than morality. His conclusion is not admonitory, but flippant: "Pudiérales decir entonces lo que un ciego a otro en Toledo, que, apartándose cada cual para su posada, dijo el uno dellos: «¡A Dios y veámonos!»" [I could have said to them then what one blind man said to another in Toledo, for, each leaving in the direction of his lodging, one of them said: "Go with God and let us see each other again soon!"] (II, 2, 8: 270). The narrative of this episode clarifies for us a more sophisticated technique of deception than that seen in the other swindles, providing a crucial disclosure of the strategy that Guzmán repeats as he pens his memoirs: deceiving with the truth. But we find no more honesty in the critical comments about his crime than before. In fact, the discursive duplicity of this last swindle achieves maximum complexity. Guzmán's diegetic commentary pursues multiple, incompatible lines of reasoning that prevent readers from assembling a consistent picture of his role in the exchange with his relatives. We are forced to form our own assessments on the basis not simply of the evidence described, but on overabundant suggestions for its interpretation that bear only oblique relation to what has happened in the narrative. In effect, the refinement of Guzmán's verbal deception in the episode we read is matched by the sophistication with which he narrates it. Both temporal planes thereby produce a common message: recipients of Guzmán's communication must consider its full potential for referentiality.

The three swindles of the narrative discussed in this section serve as attention-catching analogues for the strategy of narration that structures the extended relation of the autobiography. In depicting a process, they also anticipate culmination of his self-representation in writing. For while Guzmán's virtuosity of the *pico* (beak, mouth) enables him to enjoy considerable mobility in defining his social status within the narrative, it cannot guarantee physical confirmation of the roles he chooses. As readers learn that Guzmán's alleged "history" is mediated by stories, they find in each swindle an improvement in narrative technique: Guzmán increases his margin of safety by adding elements of truth to his fictions and by eliminating apparent discrepancies between his words and the physical reality to which they refer. In the first deal with the silversmith, Guzmán's explanatory narratives are corroborated somewhat haphazardly by the words of other soldiers who have no more knowledge of his background than does his victim. But Guzmán is dependent on the use of accomplices and physical props, which he explains to the public awkwardly. The second swindle, of the Milanese merchant, shows a *burla* that relies not simply on physical evidence and the public's acceptance of convincing narratives told by Guzmán, but upon his written imitation of legal proofs, which goes unchallenged by the very system it mocks. Unfortunately, to achieve the social effect he desires—"honor" funded by material gain—Guzmán is still dependent on accomplices and props. The third swindle most clearly approximates Guzmán's authorial technique in writing his life. Here Guzmán's victims are lured with a generally truthful account of his past and present circumstances, articulated in a context whose potential ambiguity is confusing. The *pícaro* refuses to delimit the terms their interpretation must follow, and his relatives are manipulated to create their own deception as they attempt to make sense of his words. However, once again, Guzmán must rely upon the aid of potentially untrustworthy accomplices and props, and he risks losing the material profits of the exchange, as well as severe punishment, if he is caught.

In these swindles, Guzmán's success at deceiving his audience and controlling their response is a result of his manipulative language. The stealthy alteration of physical evidence remains the most dangerous part of each deception, because it is traceable. Guzmán's security and his profit come instead from his ability to direct the public's apprehension of the physical world with a convincing parody of trusted discourses.[14] Thus, he deceives the silversmith by speaking of honor as an impoverished member of the gentry. In the swindle of the Milanese merchant he parodies judicial language to convince officials of his sincerity by creating a series of false oaths, and he misuses religious discourse to destroy his victim's reason. To rob his usurious relatives, Guzmán speaks their own language, establishing his worth and negotiating the profitable marriage that he flees. Through these communications he secures both material reward and the possibility of horizontal mobility, and the greater, immaterial reward of directing the responses of his audience within relationships that he has authored through language. He thus creates for himself figurally a "vertical" mobility literally beyond his reach.

The stories of these three swindles seem to limit the trickster's power by exposing his operations within the safe enclosure of narrative. Yet by circumscribing Guzmán's success in material "reality," they implicitly trace a much more disturbing possibility: the trickster need only deny his public access to literal, physical referents in order to work deceptions beyond their control. He does exactly that as he transforms his life into literature. As fictive author Guzmán tells us what he wants us to know of his experiences and he reflects upon them in discourses that moralize without clarifying his own culpability. In framing the narrative of each swindle, the autobiographer Guzmán is shown, despite his "present" claims to a didactic—implicitly univocal—authorial discourse, to repeat the mystifying narrational procedure seen in the narrated example of his misuse of language. Rather than contradicting the model provided with an explanation of his linguistic culpability, the narrator indicts the limited critical faculties of the victims of the language through which he positions himself in society and simultaneously guarantees the terms of his mobility. These examples of his narration, in which Guzmán brings to our attention the principles of his self-composition, reinforce the lesson related by the novel's narrated *burlas*, collapsing the distinction that critics attempt to make in the *Guzmán* between narrative "past" and narrating "present." Both temporal planes are structured upon a common discourse of concealment and disclosure, which represents not Guzmán's mutually exclusive roles as a character, but the multiple and supplementary operations of signification inherent in the language through which he composes his life.

Conclusion

Alemán's experiment with the power of writing to define its subject in the autobiography of the fictive Guzmán is structured with a complexity that received mixed reviews. In the Eulogy to Part II, Luis de Valdés conveys the applause of the scholarly and religious communities for the 1599 text as the "libro profano de mayor provecho y gusto" [the profane book of greatest benefit and pleasure] to have appeared in print (II: 25). The assessment of Valdés is clearly biased, but the booming sales of Part I (Chap. 1, n. 1) and the theorist Gracián's praise of the *Guzmán*'s conceptual brilliance well after its vogue (Chap. 3, n. 3) attest to the positive reception of Guzmán's "history" by a broad spectrum of readers—the general public and prominent men of letters alike. At the same time, the inventive autobiography of Alemán's loquacious convict met reaction by other readers, namely writers who dedicated parodies of their own to ridiculing—while at the same time profiting from—the impact made by the *Guzmán*'s serious, often arrogant wit. Quevedo's *Buscón* (written soon after Alemán's own Second Part and circulated at Court in manuscript form around 1605) and López de Ubeda's *La pícara Justina* (published 1605) ape the autobiographical format of Alemán's creation while creating narrators who are incapable of articulating weighty judgments or of being taken seriously, even by the most ignorant of readers. Other novels seeking to capitalize on the *Guzmán*'s vogue and to capture a share of the market quickly followed—Salas Barbadillo's *La hija de Celestina* (1612), Espinel's *Vida del escudero Marcos de Obregón* (1618), and Alcalá Yúñez y Rivera's *El donado hablador Alonso* (1624 and 1626) among them.

The contrast between Alemán's volumes and works by his imitators is glaring: whereas the first-person narrative of Guzmán's life defies formal or thematic classification, employing multiple, authoritative discourses with subtle shifts in modality—from serious probing to overt jest, and from diegetic editorializing to mimetic action—the stories of Justina and later *pícaros* clearly constitute *libros de entretenimiento* (jest books). The preponderance in the later works of jokes and the absence of moralizing discourse has led critics to postulate the rapid disintegration of the so-called "picaresque genre"—best exemplified by Lázaro's and Guzmán's critical assessments of self and society—into a "burlesque subgenre" that consists of the antics and misdeeds of self-ridiculing delinquents. Such readings isolate the *Guzmán*, making it an anomaly in the very trend that it precipitated. But as I have sought to demonstrate in this study, Alemán's text is very much concerned with *burlas*, at all levels of its articulation. Not only does the protagonist compose his lifestory of narrated *burlas*, indicating his tendency to both entertaining and threatening transgression of society's norms; the composition of his narration itself constitutes an extensive *burla*. Contemporary readers were invited to respond to an ever-shifting depiction of not only Guzmán's but their own reality, mediated by the words of an admitted liar. The discourse of his narration, an aggressive interpretive presence, functions in both temporal planes as obstruction to the world represented, for it suppresses the voices and opinions of those who inhabit it. Guzmán's monologic discourse, while pretending to incorporate the views of others in an implied dialogue, is instead structured on an intrinsic dialogism that enriches our perceptions only of deception, as it fragments the picture he paints of himself while confusing the reader's judgment. The fictive autobiography of Alemán's convict thus anticipates the *burlas* of later picaresque works, incorporating into the structure of its controlling narration the unstable space between *difinición* and *difinido* that they limit to *burlas* of the narrative.

The distinction between the *Guzmán de Alfarache* and its successors is not one of serious edification versus frivolous jokes, but rather of *burlas* that must be taken seriously versus ones we may discount. The important difference between Alemán's work and those of his imitators lies in the subject of power—or more accurately, the power of the subject—to determine itself linguistically. Alemán's narrator capitalizes on the figural instability of language to compose the terms of his existence in society. A diachronic series of narrations, stories of himself that he tells other characters, describe the limitations of the horizontal mobility he pursues, determined by material relationships. The synchronic writing of his life is the linguistic *burla* that aims to achieve a virtually impossible vertical mobility by eternalizing his fame. Guzmán, the convict-turned-author, is made to seek to assure his noteworthy status, or "honra," in terms of his own invention, through autobiography, arrogantly demanding recognition as a superior wit while serving time as one of his society's most infamous transgressors. Guzmán's account, which takes the form of literary expiation for his wrongs, constitutes a skillful exercise of power.

Self-righteous readers who would censure his like are compelled to praise Guzmán's criticism of vices through his example, and they must respect his astute adherence to the regulatory discourses of his contemporary society, even though the figural richness of his parody threatens the effectiveness of such discourses. Readers, in effect, are challenged to reward the concealed aggression of Guzmán, who poses as a prudent jester, or entertaining subordinate. He implicitly demands payment in timeless currency—renown—for not having stripped them of their status outright by acting as an indiscreet joker, whose effects, at least for his contemporary public, could have had more serious social implications.

As critics have rightly argued, the *Guzmán*'s successors are characterized by the *burlas* of pranksters who cannot be taken seriously, and pose no threat to the social order. In effect, there is an increasing tendency in Alemán's imitators to diminish the trickster figure's narrative authority by portraying him or her as a buffoon, clearly separating and ranking the voices of character and real author, and, in many cases, by denying the *pícaro* linguistic self-representation. The subjects of these narratives, carefully regulated and castigated performers or comics, define their relationship to society by *burlas*, but only ones that are directed by others. Just as they are stripped of power, so is the language through which they communicate. Deprivileged from its status as historiographic medium and interpreter of the material world, the figuration of language is firmly circumscribed—dedicated to entertaining, and subordinate to patronage and marketplace. In these novels, "history," posited beyond reach of the trickster's verbal artifice, is made to appear autonomous of the language through which it and its castigated *pícaro* are composed. Picaresque works of Spain's early seventeenth century appear thus to have quickly contained and trivialized the experiment in self-writing begun by Alemán in the *Guzmán de Alfarache*, thereby suggesting it to be a dangerous model for the *vulgo*—"los de nacimiento humilde"—and a presumptuous bid by its author for favor as an "admitido cortesano."

Notes

In these notes, as in the body of the study, abbreviated bibliographic references, consisting of the author's name and/or a short title, are often used. The reader is referred to the Bibliography for full citations.

INTRODUCTION

1. Various sources are cited by Rico (*Novela picaresca*, xciii–xciv) and Chevalier ("*Guzmán de Alfarache* en 1605," 146–47).
2. I am referring to these two temporal planes of utterance in the sense detailed in Emile Benveniste's chapter "Tense in the French Verb" (*Problems in General Linguistics*, 206). While their distribution is complementary in the *Guzmán*, this study will trace a common rhetorical function in conveying the narrative's exemplarity.
3. See Chapter 1, note 5.
4. The citation occurs in the final line of the dedicatory poem to the 1630 edition of Mabbe's translation, *The rogue*: "So that none/Can better teach by worse meanes; who by strange/Bifronted posture, ill, to good doth change."
5. References to studies of religious heterodoxy and moral ambiguity in the *Guzmán* are found in Chapter 1, note 6. Analyses of a broader sociocritical focus are cited in note 7 of the same chapter.
6. Since the Spanish term encompasses multiple types of deceptive behavior wrought with intellectual cunning—pranks, insults, hoaxes, jests, jokes, swindles, and so forth—I will use *burla* when referring to this type of social interaction, rather than a reductive English translation.
7. All translations of quotations from the *Guzmán* and other works, unless otherwise specified, are mine. I have opted not to use the translation of James Mabbe, although it renders the tenor of the *Guzmán*'s language with greater accuracy for the period and decidedly more eloquence, because Mabbe made many deletions and alterations in translating Alemán's original text, often eliminating the segments of importance to my own discussion.
8. In "Relaciones de dependencia," Maravall consigns the function of the *gracioso* and that of the *pícaro* to the separate literary forms, respectively, of the *comedia* and prose narrative. His *La literatura picaresca desde la historia social* concentrates primarily on the radically marginated status of the *pícaro* figure in prose, its social causes and widespread literary manifestations. His treatment of the *Guzmán*'s extraliterary context offers considerable insight into the work's composition, but I find his reading of the *pícaro*'s literary function to be reductive. Both the functions of *gracioso* and of *pícaro* coalesce in the *Guzmán*, a narrative whose argument works toward the affirmation of established values and the questioning of the same. As Sieber suggests in his discussion of the *Lazarillo* (*Language and Society*), the motive for the narrator's astute performance as *homo litteratus* exceeds that of the desire for physical sus-

tenance or independence from social bonds. The desire for praise of his literary creation, as Rico agrees ("Para el Prólogo del *Lazarillo*," 115–16), drives the narrator to perform like the *truhán* (jester) cited in the Prologue itself. The purpose of my own study is to show that the *Guzmán* also suggests a context of reception in which the narrator seeks reward for his entertaining narrative confirmation of the readers' superiority, while he simultaneously hints that their status is a product of narration itself.

9. Because the term *discretos* is defined ambiguously within the *Guzmán* for the purposes of narrative strategy, I will use the Spanish term with its multiple connotations rather than reduce it to a single English interpretation.

10. Citing testimony of real *pícaros*, Carrillo ("La vida del pícaro," and *Semiolinguística de la picaresca*) argues that the literary picaresque is the expression of cultural rather than material margination on the part primarily of *conversos*. The critic suggests ("La vida del pícaro," 365) that picaresque narrative systematically constitutes an intellectual posture of *burla* upon the traditional concept of honor and, hence, Spain's feudal caste system.

11. Benveniste's Chapters 20 and 21 in *Problems in General Linguistics* ("The Nature of Pronouns" and "Subjectivity in Language") analyze in depth the relational capacities of discourse.

12. In so doing, I am rejecting Rico's theory (*Punto de vista*) of the narrative's importance as negative *exempla* that motivate the narrator's ideological reversal in the present. I also take issue with Ife's more recent assertions (*Reading and Fiction in Golden-Age Spain*) that the narrative submits readers to experiential deception clarified by his authorial discourse. Both will be discussed further in the chapters to follow.

Chapter 1. The "Figure" Guzman

1. Claudio Guillén (*Literature as System*, 143) observes that "*Guzmán de Alfarache* was one of the first authentic best sellers in the history of printing," and that, in fact, "its huge success immediately transformed a narrative form . . . into a convention." For extensive catalogues of the many editions and translations of Alemán's work, see Ricapito's *Bibliografía razonada*, and Laurenti's *Bibliografía* and *Suplemento*.

2. Examples of the earliest translations are Aegidius Albertinus's *Der Landstörtzer Gusman von Alfarache oder Picaro gennant* (1615); G. Chappuys's *Le Gueux, ou la vie de Guzman d'Alfarache* (1621); Gabriel Brémond's *Histoire de l'admirable Don Guzman d'Alfarache* (1695); James Mabbe's *The rogue: or, The life of Guzman de Alfarache* (1622).

3. Imitations of the *Guzmán* in translation include Hans Jakob Christoffel von Grimmelshausen's *Der abentheuerliche Simplicissimus Teutsch* (1668), Richard Head's *The English Rogue* (1665–80), Daniel Defoe's *The Fortunes and Misfortunes of Moll Flanders* (1722), and Alain Lesage's *Histoire de Gil Blas de Santillane* (1732).

4. Early examples are Chandler's famous study, *The Literature of Roguery*, and less-known texts such as Salillas's, *Hampa (antropología picaresca)* and Zarandieta Mirabent's *El "golfo" en la novela picaresca y el "golfo" en Madrid*. Ricapito's bibliography provides an exhaustive list of studies at the beginning of the twentieth century in both areas.

5. This trend is represented by Moreno Báez's *Lección y sentido del* Guzmán de Alfarache, which develops ideas expressed earlier by Herrero in "Nueva interpretación de la novela picaresca." See also Valbuena Prat's Prologue to his edition of the *Guzmán* in *La novela picaresca española*; Blanco Aguinaga, "Cervantes y la picaresca"; Parker, *Literature and the Delinquent*; McGrady, *Mateo Alemán*; Rico, ed., *La*

novela picaresca española, cviii–cli; idem, "Estructuras y reflejos de estructuras;" and idem, *La novela picaresca y el punto de vista.* Dunn ("Cervantes De/Reconstructs the Picaresque") reminds us, however, that readings by Spanish intellectuals of the *Guzmán* as an authoritarian text during this period may have contemporary ideological motives, and should be considered in the context of the Franco era (116–17, n. 10). Michaud's recent book, *Mateo Alemán, moraliste chrétien* (1987), a detailed and exhaustive study, expands upon Moreno Báez's thesis, tracing the vast network of intertextual relationships between the narrator's moralizing statements and argumentation of an explicitly theological or religious nature from other texts. However, in my opinion, there is sufficient lexical dissimilarity between many examples to distinguish the enunciations of the *pícaro* and problematize the articulation of doctrinal concerns through his voice. Russell ("English Seventeenth-Century Interpretations," 73) provides interesting insights into the question of how such references were received by English readers of Mabbe's translation. According to him, the fact that Mabbe did not emend the work's religious references to suit the Protestant taste of English readers, despite the widespread practice of such alterations in a country of anti-Catholic sentiment, and the fact that the work escaped criticism to become a best-seller in England suggest that the *Guzmán* was not perceived to be a Tridentine apology. Dunn (*The Spanish Picaresque,* 61) argues convincingly that Alemán's work supports both a Catholic and a generally didactic reading: "We may see it either as Guzmán's life, expanded and universalized by the intellectual framework of the commentaries, or as an expiation, a rhetorical assault upon human life illustrated by the experience of the picaro."

6. They include Castro, *Hacia Cervantes,* 118–42; idem, *De la edad conflictiva,* 188–89; van Praag, "El sentido de *Guzmán*"; Bataillon, "Les nouveaux chrétiens"; Nagy, "El anhelo de Guzmán"; del Monte, *Itinerario de la novela picaresca,* 76–96; Silverman, "Literature and Life in the Golden Age"; Asensio, "En torno a Américo Castro," 380–83; Sicroff, "Américo Castro," 9–15; Agüera, "Salvación del cristiano nuevo"; Arias, *Unrepentant Narrator;* Bjornson, "Apologia for a 'Converso'"; idem, "*Guzmán* and the *Converso* Problem" in *The Picaresque Hero;* Norval, "Original Sin and the 'Conversion'"; Johnson, *Inside Guzmán;* Brancaforte, ed., *Guzmán de Alfarache,* 17–51; *¿Conversión o proceso de degradación?;* idem, "Juez-penitente"; Rodríguez, "La poética del gracioso"; idem, *El narrador pícaro;* and Whitenack, *Impenitent Confession.*

7. Examples include the following works by Cros: *Protée et le gueux; Mateo Alemán,* 95–109 and 129–44; "Prédication carcérale"; and *Sociocriticism,* particularly Chapters 10 and 11. See also Molho, *Introducción al pensamiento picaresco,* 59–118; Cavillac, *Gueux et marchands;* Guerreiro, "A propos de origines de Guzmán"; and his "Honra, jerarquía social y pesimismo."

8. Elbaz particularly refers to theorists who share his interest in contextualizing study of autobiography within a "dynamic" (3) or intersubjective process. Of that group he takes issue with Bruss (*Autobiographical Acts*) and Lejeune (*Le Pacte autobiographique*), who argue for the historical or materialist basis of autobiography.

9. Howarth ("Some Principles of Autobiography," 365) argues that autobiographical narrative is inherently fictive by virtue of its very composition through narration: "Autobiography is thus hardly 'factual,' 'unimaginative,' or even 'nonfictional,' for it welcomes all the devices of skilled narration and observes few of the restrictions—accuracy, impartiality, inclusiveness—imposed upon other forms of historical literature." It seems to me, therefore, unnecessary to designate the *Guzmán* as "pseudo-autobiography."

10. Sobejano, "De Alemán a Cervantes," 729.

11. Delgado Gómez ("El lector del *Guzmán*") concurs with Peale ("*Guzmán de Alfarache* como discurso oral") in his assessment of the *Guzmán*'s narration as oral discourse. In his study of what he considers to be the work's dialogic structure, Delgado Gómez points out (91) that the reader is forced to assume the oscillating roles of a simply "curious" reader, an "interlocutor," and a "long-suffering listener" to moralizing harangues.

12. In the next paragraph of the Declaración (I: 89), Alemán attributes the fictive author's crimes specifically to bad company and idle time.

13. My views on Alemán's Prologues differ from those of Laurenti (*Los prólogos*, 25), who argues against any emergence in the narrative of the author's implied personal relationship with readers. The relationship that I see, however, has been figuratively constructed.

14. Rodríguez Marín, *Documentos*, 194.

15. Accounts of Alemán's economic problems and of his conflicts with superiors while serving as a royal bureaucrat may be found in the biographies of Cros and McGrady; for more on these and other aspects of his checkered career and social fortunes see also Bleiberg, "Mateo Alemán y los galeotes" and *Informe secreto*; Guillén, "Los pleitos extremeños"; and Cros, "Deux épîtres inédites" and "La vie de Mateo Alemán."

16. Riley, *Cervantes's Theory of the Novel*, 108; Green, "The *vulgo* in the Spanish *Siglo de Oro*," 196–200; Cruickshank, "Literature and the Booktrade," 818–24.

17. Tratado 7 reveals details of the *ménage-à-trois* that Lázaro has been commanded to explain to "uno" (one)—"Vuestra Merced" (Your Grace)—at the same time that he strives to keep the information from becoming general knowledge and an item of conversation around town, among "muchos," or the general public. The fictive author of the *Lazarillo* clearly capitalizes in the composition of his account upon the unequal intellect and training attributed to these two sectors of the reading public, for his disclosure of the truth finds expression in figural language that conceals what it refers to from the general public. For more on the rhetorical design of the novel, see Sieber's *Language and Society*; Carey, "Quest for Authority"; Shipley, "The Critic as Witness"; and his "Not a Hardworking, Clean-Living Water Carrier."

18. Riley observes (*Cervantes's Theory of the Novel*, 114) that there was actually no clear division of the reading public into a "scholarly" and an "ignorant" class. Readers of novels fell into "a leisured, literate class . . . between the extremes of the *discretos* and the *vulgo*.

19. *Diccionario de autoridades*, s.v. *lascivo*, defines the term, generally, as a lack of restraint or excessive indulgence in sensuality: "Por Antónomasia se entiende la persona propensa à la sensualidad. . . ."

20. See Davis, "Style of Mateo Alemán's *Guzmán*," 204, for a discussion of ellipsis/zeugma and ironic or antithetical expressions as "a distinct stylistic trait" of Guzmán's narrative; also Brancaforte's introduction to his edition of the *Guzmán*, 36.

21. All references to the *Lazarillo* are taken from this edition.

22. Rico maintains ("Para el Prólogo del *Lazarillo*," 101) that the linguistic polysemia of the narrator's examples, which proceed from the sublime to the ridiculous, implies not only that Lázaro's own honor is degraded, but that the honor of those whom he emulates is no better.

23. The term occurs in noun and adjective form in the *Lazarillo*, on 199, 201, and 202.

24. Miller (*Picaresque Novel*, 56–57) argues against the attribution of realist or objective status to the narrator Guzmán, noting that "having become a manipulator

of appearances, the picaresque character Guzmán settles into the non-reality of becoming an appearance himself." Américo Castro (*Hacia Cervantes*, 83–84) assesses the "figuras" through which Guzmán portrays himself and others similarly: "Se adivinan las zarabandas y retorcimientos del Bosco, con figuras que hacen dudar la autenticidad de cuanto se contempla" [One divines the debaucheries and writhings of Bosch, in figures that cast doubt on the authenticity of all that is before the eye].

25. Stephen Greenblatt explores the implications of what he refers to as "narrative self-fashioning" in a number of provocative articles and book-length studies on literature of the English Renaissance. His arguments should bear consideration for the context of Golden Age Spanish literature as well. See, for example, "Improvisation and Power" in *Literature and Society* (reproduced in *Renaissance Self-Fashioning*), and his more recent *Representing the English Renaissance*.

26. This definition finds fuller discussion in Quevedo's listing of types of *figuras* in *Vida de corte*, circulated in manuscript form probably during the year that Alemán's Part I appeared. See "Obras festivas," in *Obras completas* I.

27. Brancaforte points out in his notes (I: 118, n. 105) that use by men of the *copete* was considered in Spain to be a "vil afeminamiento" (vile effeminacy) and was prohibited in years following publication of the *Guzmán*.

28. Henri Guerreiro's analysis in "Honra, jerarquía social y pesimismo" of the discourse on honor in Part II, 1, 3–4 reveals that Alemán has Guzmán repeat this extraliterary focus of the narrative's opening pages with a much more prolonged attack on the decadence of the nobility and corruption of justice officials in Part II, as well. Guerreiro argues that Alemán's intention in both sections is not to establish a negative moral determinism for his protagonist, but to criticize specific historical groups responsible for exploiting the condition of his likes.

29. According to definitions of honor by Castro (*De la edad conflictiva*, 69, 193) the fictive author hopes to acquire for himself the *honor* or virtue normally considered inherent in elevated social rank through the *honra*—fame and preferred treatment—that his literary work will bring him. Arias (*Unrepentant Narrator*, 14) discusses the distinction but denies the fictive author's ability to win honor for himself in any terms. See also San Miguel (*Sentido y estructura*, 163), who summarizes the definitions of honor accordingly: *honor* as "honra-virtud" (honor-virtue) and *honra* as "honra-opinión" (honor-opinion).

30. Rico's *La novela picaresca y el punto de vista* is at the forefront of readings of this type, but most recent critics discuss the problem in the course of their studies. For discussion of the perspective of the narrator in the character or vice versa, see Rico (*Punto de vista*, especially 69–72); McGrady, *Mateo Alemán*, 95; and Parker, *Literature and the Delinquent*, 36. Readings opposed to a singular "point of view" include Jones, "Duality and Complexity," 32; Rey, "La novela picaresca y el narrador fidedigno," 60–63; and Peale, "*Guzmán de Alfarache* como discurso oral," 25–57.

31. See also Riggan, 172; Folkenflik, 353.

32. The narrator's discourse is heteroglossic in the Bakhtinian sense, but I have chosen to refer to it in subsequent sections in architectural terms because, in the course of his self-representation, Guzmán invokes and alters a series of power relationships that have spatial—particularly vertical—dimension. Bakhtin's *The Dialogic Imagination* and *Rabelais and his World* are important reference works for this study. My working concept of discourse is also indirectly informed by Foucault's works, particularly *The Archeology of Knowledge* and *Discipline and Punish*.

33. Reed (*Exemplary History of the Novel*, 59–60) argues that the symbolic act of punishment that structures the *Guzmán* is manifested by the castigation Guzmán receives for his delinquency. According to him, the focus of this process is the *pícaro* or individual, rather than society. Paulson ("Fool-Knave Relation in Picaresque

Satire," 78) argues that power relationships in this process of castigation are determined not by social institution and norms of behavior, but by "superior cunning or strength or luck."

34. Arias's study, particularly Chapters I, II, and IV, provides an excellent analysis of the limitations posed for readers by the *Guzmán*'s autobiographical format. Our studies differ considerably, however, in the assessments made of Guzmán's discourse as author; while it is my contention that the subject articulates more than one discourse for the purpose of forging a complex social relationship with his readers, Arias finds that he narrates from the unchanged, singular "point of view" of an unrepentant wrongdoer whose disillusionment with the world results in his pessimistic isolation. For Guzmán's control of perspective through autobiography, see also Ayala (151) and Friedman (124).

35. Hilary Smith ("The *pícaro* Turns Preacher," 394) sees the shifting perspectives of the narrator as Alemán's principal innovation: "The originality of the *Guzmán de Alfarache* is that its narrator-protagonist is alternately 'up there' and 'down below,' observer and observed."

36. Juan Martí's continuation, *Segunda parte de la vida del pícaro Guzmán de Alfarache*, appeared under the pseudonym Matheo Luxán de Sayavedra, in Valencia, 1602.

37. The use of the imperfect indicative "venía" in this passage is troubling, but the following use of the imperfect subjunctive in "mandase" clarifies that the decree had not yet officially been granted. The former verb thus seems to be one of indirect discourse, an allusion to the words of the captain regarding the pending status of the requested commutation.

38. McGrady (*Mateo Alemán*, 44) views the *pícaro* figure as a composite of three literary types: the wanderer, have-not, and jester. In McGrady's opinion, however, Guzmán's humor bears no relationship to his didactic function.

39. Deleito y Piñuela (*El rey se divierte*, 121–29) cites jesters as common members of royal households in Europe through the seventeenth century. Although he cites examples from the period of Felipe IV, Deleito's descriptions show the extraliterary basis of Alemán/Guzmán's discourse on the importance of jester figures as advisers to the powerful. Deleito characterizes "bufones" (buffoons) as outspoken, even insolent with their patrons, and well rewarded for their wit.

40. *Diccionario de autoridades*, s.v. *chocarrero*, defines this figure in functional terms in the same way that it defines *juglar* or *gracioso*. *Chocarrero* (vulgar comic) is "el bufón, truhán y placentéro, que siempre habla de burlas, para hacer reir à otros, sin tener otro empléo ni exercicio" [the buffoon, knavish rascal and entertainer, who always speaks in jest to make others laugh, without having any other employment or exercise]. *Juglar* (jester) is "el que entretiene con burlas y donáires, que mas comunmente se llama truhan ò bufon" [he who entertains with jokes and witticisms, who is more commonly called a knavish rascal or buffoon]. And *gracioso* (comic) is "chistoso, agudo, lleno de donáire y gracia" (jesting, clever, full of pleasing wit and charm), "inclinado à hacer grácias" (given to please with his performance). In this study, I have chosen to use the term *juglar* (jester), rather than *gracioso* (comic) or others, to indicate this function of Guzmán, for the reasons explained in my Introduction.

41. The function of Guzmán in these two roles and its relation to the narrative of the last novel in the genre, *Estebanillo González*, is the subject of my article, "The *Pícaro* as Jester in the Spanish Picaresque," which sketches the direction of a longer study that I am currently undertaking of discursive functions in various works of the picaresque genre.

Chapter 2. Guzman's History

1. Analyzing the temporally disjunctive link between the work's narrative and moralizing discourse, anecdotes, novellas, and other materials that interrupt it, Ricapito ("Two Editors and the Structure of *Guzmán de Alfarache*," 17) interprets suspension of temporal logic in the overall framework of Alemán's work as indication of the narrator Guzmán's conversion: "Once a form of spiritual salvation has been achieved . . . there is a suspension of the tension that directs and governs the life." He argues that Guzmán "seems to have settled down to an extended moment, an eternal moment of recollection." As Chapters 2 and 3 of this study will clarify, I do not agree with his interpretation. This chapter focuses only on problems of temporal sequencing within the narrative itself.

2. Lucas Gracián Dantisco's work, *Galateo español* (1590), provides a descriptive catalogue of jesting *burlas*, in the form of "motes" (riddles) and "befas" (jeers) employed in extraliterary communication during the period of the *Guzmán*'s composition. He observes (ed. Morreale, 148–49) that although riddles and jokes were instruments of laughter and recreation, certain riddles were objectionably mordant and damaging. There is a thin line between the entertainment and serious embarrassment produced by *burlas*, and the effects depend upon the power relationship between speaker and recipient.

3. In his review article of *Language and Society* ("The Life and Adventures of Cipión") González Echevarría takes issue (18) with Sieber's book for similar procedure, but it is clearly warranted by the rhetoric that develops the lifestory.

4. See Maravall's complex analysis of this motivation in the picaresque genre, as reflection of social phenomenon, in Chapter 8 of *La literatura picaresca* ("La aspiración de medro como fenómeno social").

5. The moral determinism of the *Guzmán* is discussed by Rico in *Punto de vista* (82) and "Estructuras y reflejos" (173–75). See also Blanco Aguinaga (317–18 and 326).

6. Maravall asserts ("The Diphasic Schema of a Social Crisis," 16–18) that while "ascendent vertical mobility" or actual change of social rank was a limited phenomenon in Golden Age Spain, the increase of both "horizontal" (geographical) and "professional" (or occupational) mobility heralded modernization. He maintains (18) that the *pícaro* figure exemplifies both of the latter movements; as my argument will clarify, I suggest that this figure enunciates an attempt to bridge the gap to the former, more desirable shift in status figuratively, in the composition of his autobiography.

7. The juxtaposition of "cosas" (things) and "honrosas" (honorable) is in itself oxymoronic, if we consider that "cosas" suppresses reference to social deviancy in the *Lazarillo* and many places in the *Guzmán*.

8. Eoff ("Picaresque Psychology," 114–15) is one of the few critics to recognize the importance of the fictive author's quest for honor as a motivating force in the narrative. He observes: "In short, the 'psychological' story of Guzmán is that of a person who, heavily conditioned by his environment, aspires always to a comfortable and privileged position in society, resorts to subterfuge as a means of attaining his goal, rationalizes his moral disorderliness in the name of necessity and current social practices, develops pride in his expert chicanery as compensation for his inferiority, and reaches eventually a culminating point of greed, shamelessness, and buffoonery. . . . Guzmán is not interested in seeing the social order changed; he merely wishes to change his position within the order."

9. In addition to drawing attention to the linguistic source of his honor, Guzmán's reference to "crowing" prefigures his adult function as a preacherly author. *Diccionario de autoridades*, s.v. *gallo*, adds: ". . . el symbolo del gallo . . . significa los perlados de la Yglesia y los predicadores, con cuya dotrina se han de reduzir los malos . . ." [. . . the symbol of the cock . . . signifies the prelates of the Church and the preachers, with whose doctrine the evil are to reduce themselves to God's authority . . .].

10. Bakhtin's *Rabelais and His World* offers a detailed analysis of the social function of carnival motifs in early modern literature, using the Rabelaisian text as a paradigm. The inversion of the power relationship between king and fool is particularly pertinent to the *Guzmán* and other picaresque works.

11. The reference to "muchos del tusón" is an ironic commentary upon activity that "florecía" at Court. *Diccionario de autoridades* (s.v. *tusón*) clarifies that the exclusive order admitted few members: "es sin duda este Orden uno de los mas célebres, è insignes, que se han establecido, por la grandeza, y singularidad de los Principes, y Señores, que solo se admiten en él" [without doubt this Order is one of the most renowned and distinguished that has been established, on account of the greatness and singularity of Princes and Lords, for they alone are admitted to it]. See also Brancaforte's edition, I: 255, n. 33. *Potro*, a synonym for *tusón*, lists among its definitions the "rack" upon which wrongdoers are tortured, suggesting a possible word play in reference both to the possessors of hereditary "honor" and to those in pursuit of a facade of "honra" through illegal means. This is intensified by the additional meaning of *tusona* (*Diccionario de autoridades*, s.v. *tusona*), "Ramera, ò dama Cortesana. Pudo decirse assi, porque les cortan el pelo por castigo, ò ellas le pierden por el vicio deshonesto" [Whore or courtesan. It could be thus said because they cut their hair for punishment, or they (the whores) lose it from illicit vice].

12. "El me pareció un ángel: tal se me representó su cara como la del deseado médico al enfermo" [He seemed to me an angel: his face represented itself to me as that of the physician desired by the sick man] (I, 1, 4: 156). This reference anticipates Guzmán's designation at the novel's end of the boatswain who is in charge of slaves as an "ángel de guarda" (guardian angel) (II, 3, 8:454). The narrator's use of "angel" to refer to earthly benefactors who contribute to his well-being clearly indicates that the meaning of his words derives from context, not discursive register.

13. The topic of the narrative's variety as a banquet designed to please many palates is invoked several times in the *Guzmán*. The fictive author complains particularly about the difficulty in pleasing readers' tastes at the beginning of Part II (II, 1, 1: 41).

14. Abbreviated segments of the first two sections of this chapter are incorporated in my article, "Indigestion and Edification."

15. In his "Guzmán y el cocinero o del estilo de servir a principes" (137–39), Guerreiro traces the character of the entrepreneurial court cook in several literary sources of the period, arguing that the figure functions as an index of corruption in the dominant political hierarchy.

16. Guzmanillo's servitude extends to his compliance during off hours in distasteful physical activities at the insistence of his immediate superiors, pages and serving boys, a possible foreshadowing of his physical service to the boatswain, according to the latter's desires, near the novel's end: "Cuando en casa no había quehacer, . . . En mí hacían anatomía, otras veces para probarme hicieron cebaderos, poniéndome moneda donde forzosamente hubiese de dar con ella" [When there were no house chores, . . . they played doctor with me, other times to test me

they made storage piles, putting coins in me where I unavoidably had to produce them] (I, 2, 5: 296–97).

17. Cañedo ("El 'curriculum vitae' del pícaro," 135–43) identifies *ingenio* (ingenuity, genius) as an important motivating force in the *Guzmán*, finding an inverse relationship between the *pícaro*'s servitude as a "boy of many masters" and his use of "ingenio" to create his own position in society. According to his statistical analysis, references to the character's servitude to others diminish as the narrative progresses, whereas the focus on his inventive genius increases (159). San Miguel (*Sentido y estructura*, 211–12) goes a step further, suggesting that the *ingenio* of Guzmán's communication informs the aesthetic of his narrative as an important structuring principle.

18. Eoff's argument supports my reading of this pattern; he maintains (112) that the *burla* is one of the primary means through which the protagonist "builds up his pride in competition with others."

19. *Diccionario de autoridades* (s.v. *papagayo*) elaborates the parallel between the communication of parrots and jesters in the following terms: "Hablar como el papagayo . . . vale decir algunas cosas buenas y discretas, sin inteligencia ni conocimiento" [To speak like the parrot . . . means to say certain good and prudent things, without intelligence or knowledge].

20. Joly (62–63) also cites the distinction in the *Guzmán* between classes of jokes, designating them "graciosa burla" (witty joke) and "burla pesada" (damaging joke). However, we disagree about what constitutes the former; for Joly, only monetary and sexual *burlas* are "pesadas," while those played upon Nicolao and the ambassador's guests are "graciosas," although they constitute social dishonor in the form of severe public embarrassment. It is my opinion that the definition of *burlas pesadas* strictly in modern, materialist terms overlooks the concept of honor operative during the period; while the physical loss of money or other heavily valorized items clearly constituted a *burla pesada*, so could figurative diminishment of the victim's stature.

21. Sobejano ("De la intención y valor," 274) finds, in Guzmán's disdain of the solution sought by Lazarillo, Alemán's deliberate intent to depict his protagonist as superior in genius to that of the anonymous narrative.

22. This *burla*, in effect, inverts the technique of a *tropelía*, or sleight-of-hand trick, playing against audience expectations of the latter type of deception. Woodward ("El casamiento engañoso y el *Coloquio de los perros*," 82, 84), describes a *tropelía* as an apparent or visible modification in substance or a "fake transformation" that results from trickery rather than any substantive change. Guzmanillo makes a real alteration in content, which is not perceptible in the context of his performance.

23. Oakley ("Problematic Unity of the *Guzmán*," 206) sees Guzmán's work with the cardinal and ambassador in the middle of his life as representative of the "two poles between which he oscillates"—the former embodying Grace and Virtue, and the latter symbolic of self-interest. Joly (301–2), however, suspects an elliptical commentary on the true nature of the cardinal, for the injurious *burlas* played on Nicolao are not censured by the prelate, but treated as amusement.

24. See Rico's discussion of the episode and Guzmán's "brilliant synthesis" in the polysemia of this expression, in "Estructuras y reflejos" (178–80).

25. Gracián Dantisco (ed. Morreale, 148) cautions that because they may lead to hostile responses, most types of *burlas* should be worked only by professional jokers: "Y aunque sea assí que los motes y burlas suelen ser bien recebidos, no le aconsejaría yo al plático gentilhombre se diesse mucho a ellos. . . . Porque bien mirado, los motes no son otra cosa más que ardides y engaños sotiles. Y assí . . . dévese dexar a los que viven dello, que aunque más os digan, no os puede perjudicar, antes merecen

ser premiados si dizen graciosamente. Pero quando el gentilhombre galateo dize alguna agudeza, considere que a cada uno le duele de que le digan su falta ni error. Y assí por muchas causas parece que quien procura ser bienquisto no se deve hazer maestro de befas, y mucho menos se precie de dezir dichos satíricos y escandalosos, siendo como son perjudiciales, aunque sean más agudos y graciosos . . ." [And although it may be that riddles and jokes are usually well received, I would not advise the politic gentleman to devote himself much to them. . . . For, carefully examined, riddles are nothing more than tricks and subtle deceptions. And so . . . they should be left to those who live by it, for however often they may say them to you, they cannot harm you; rather, they deserve to be rewarded if they speak wittily. But when the courtly gentleman says some sharp witticism, consider that in each case, one is pained to hear his lack or error broadcast. And thus, for many reasons, it seems that he who aspires to being well-liked should not become a master of insults and even less take pride in speaking scandalous and satirical sayings, being as they are damaging, even though they may be witty and entertaining . . .].

26. *Diccionario de autoridades*, s.v. *barloventear*, gives: "Puntear ù dár bordos el navío quando no tiene viento favorable para navegar, à fin de ponerse sobre el viento" [For the ship to tack when it doesn't have favorable wind for navigating, with the objective of placing itself into the wind] and "Metaphoricamente es andar de una parte à otra sin firmeza ni estabilidád" [Metaphorically it is to go from one part to another without firmness or stability]; s.v. *echar la llave*, "Vale lo mismo que Cerrar" [It means the same as to close]. Guzmán evidently articulates a play on *cerrar* and the literal meaning of the individual words that compose the expression, *echar* and *llave*.

27. See Chapter 1, notes 5 and 6.

28. These relationships undertaken to gain preferential treatment while serving time as slave, and the final articulation of his bid for favor from the bowels of the ship, as *corullero*, are the subject of my article, "Confidence and the *corullero*."

29. Longhurst asserts (101) that the narrator's expression of a desire for spiritual emendation, in this context, must be seen not as evidence of conviction but rather as a last-ditch attempt to save himself. His thorough review (91–101) of sixteenth-century conceptions of conversion presents very convincing evidence that the narrator's experience would not have been perceived by Alemán's readers as having constituted any of the three basic types.

CHAPTER 3. GUZMAN TELLS HIS STORY

1. See my Introduction.

2. Marin (*Interruption-Resumption in Autobiography*, 101–11) argues that Benveniste's temporal distinctions have no real function in autobiographical writing; the illusion of temporality is created by systematic self-interruption of an essentially achronic (that is, synchronic) authorial discourse, as it shifts modes of narration, implicitly between diegesis and mimesis. Through these repetitive interruptions of his own utterance, the narrator both describes how he came to be and simultaneously performs the ontic function of creating the being of whom he speaks.

3. Gracián cites Alemán's book as an outstanding example of the use of *agudeza* to create compound wit in extended argumentation, "agudeza compuesta" or "agudeza mayor," in *Agudeza y arte de ingenio*, 364, 372–73, 435, 477–79, 482, 508; and in *El criticón*, 875, 1143.

4. In my opinion, Alemán's novel exemplifies the transitional culture that Godzich and Spadaccini ("Popular Culture and Spanish Literary History") have termed "auditive" (that is, between oral and written culture). It is highly rhetorical, inven-

tive, and, in their words (47), "does not seek to establish a dialogical relation with the audience but instead to leave the audience dumbfounded: *boca abierta.*"

5. See *Figures* III: 222, for Genette's discussion of rhetorical tropes and figures typical of the literary period of the *Guzmán*, with which the medium of narration could be made to render its message ambiguous.

6. Fish argues (*Self-Consuming Artifacts*, 386) that the narrative strategy of promising information and not providing it, or offering information and then obscuring its meaning, is an identifying feature of Baroque prose. In analyzing narrative of this literary period, readers must consider not only the content but also the medium of statements made, to determine their function in the work's context: "Whatever is persuasive and illuminating about this analysis . . . is the result of my substituting for one question—what does this sentence mean?—another, more operational question—what does this sentence do? And what the sentence does is give the reader something and then take it away, drawing him on with the unredeemed promise of its return. An observation about the sentence as an utterance—its refusal to yield a declarative statement—has been transformed into an account of its experience (not being able to get a fact out of it)." Croll ("Baroque Style," 26–52), provides an analysis of the "curt" style in Baroque prose that sheds light on one of the *Guzmán*'s most recurrent patterns: he notes that the narrative is structured on a long series of passages that are intended to give the impression of progression, but in fact repeat the same idea in many different ways. Guzmán's history of *burlas* essentially exhibits this composition, for the only development in its series of similar communications is one of refinement.

7. In Babcock's terms, the *pícaro*'s narrative confuses normally opposed categories and employs multiple codes to create conflicting expectations on the part of readers: "the effect of such masking, transformation, and inversion as is characteristic of the picaresque is to render ambiguous or 'nondisjunctive' (as Kristeva terms it) primary categories which are usually distinguished, such as good and evil. . . . Nondisjunction both of meaning and of formal generic constraints—that is, the coexistence of two or more metacode signals and thus of several sets of expectations—also contributes to the 'problematic' ending characteristic of the picaresque" ("Liberty's a Whore," 110–11).

8. The analysis of the swindles that follows forms the argument of my article, "Guzmán('s) Swindles."

9. San Miguel (211–23) discusses the caper with the Milanese merchant; Johnson (36–40) also comments on this episode; and Guzmán's swindle of his relatives is analyzed by Cortázar (93–95).

10. *Diccionario de autoridades*, s.v. *doblón*, lists numerous types of *doblones*: "de a ciento" (of one hundred), "de a ocho" (of eight), and "de a cuatro" (of four). Their assigned value evidently changed continually, but they are defined comparatively by their weight in gold (e.g., the *doblón de a ocho* coin was equivalent in weight to four simple *doblones*). The *doblón de a cuatro* is referred to as a rare coin and there is no entry for "doblones de a diez," indicating either its greater scarcity or Alemán's own joke on the readers.

11. In his analysis of this swindle, San Miguel observes that the readers themselves risk being deceived by the ambiguities of the narrative, in a battle of wits whose pleasure is purely intellectual (222–23). Arias (41–42) shows that Guzmán also transfers blame following the Milanese swindle to a more general adversary designated "others."

12. Johnson (36–40) discusses the notable absence of the autocritical focus that readers expect to find here. Instead, Guzmán presents the effects of his genius as a

triumph, a pleasure-causing mastery that is designed to impress the readers favorably. Johnson terms this vital component the "titillation aspect" (32).

13. The convict-turned-author's words suggest in passing that the justice meted out to "los pobres pecadores como yo" constitutes another indication of excess on the part of their superiors; he includes himself in what is at this point in the narrative an enigmatic allusion to those sentenced to hanging: "Un ladrón, ¿qué no hará por hurtar? Digo ladrón a los pobres pecadores como yo; que con los ladrones de bien, con los que arrastran gualdrapas de terciopelo, con los que revisten sus paredes con brocadas y cubren el suelo con oro y seda turquí, con los que nos ahorcan a nosotros, no hablo . . ." [A thief, what will he not do to steal? I say "thief" of poor sinners like myself; of affluent thieves, those who trail velvet trappings, those who cover their walls with brocades and cover the floor with gold and Turkish silk, those who hang us, I speak not . . .] (II, 2, 7: 237).

14. B. Davis ("The Style of Mateo Alemán's *Guzmán*," 206) lists the many "specialized vocabularies" that the fictive author uses to direct our perceptions of his persona.

Bibliography

Agüera, Victorio. "Salvación del cristiano nuevo en el *Guzmán de Alfarache*." *Hispania* 57 (1974):23–30.

Arias, Joan. *Guzmán de Alfarache: The Unrepentant Narrator*. London: Tamesis, 1977.

Asensio, Eugenio. "En torno a Américo Castro. Polémica con Albert A. Sicroff." *Hispanic Review* 40 (1972):365–85.

Ayala, Francisco. *Experiencia e invención*. Madrid: Taurus, 1970.

Babcock, Barbara A. "'Liberty's a Whore': Inversions, Marginalia, and Picaresque Narrative." In *The Reversible World*, edited by Barbara A. Babcock, 95–116. Ithaca: Cornell Univ. Press, 1978.

Bakhtin, Mikhail. *The Dialogic Imagination*. Translated by Caryl Emerson and Michael Holquist. Edited by Michael Holquist. Austin: Univ. of Texas Press, 1981.

———. *Rabelais and His World*. Translated by Helene Iswolsky. Cambridge: M.I.T. Press, 1978.

Barthes, Roland. "An Introduction to the Structural Analysis of Narrative." *New Literary History* 6 (1974):237–72.

Bataillón, Marcel. "Les nouveaux chrétiens dans l'essor du roman picaresque." *Neophilologus* 4 (1974):283–98.

Benveniste, Emile. *Problems in General Linguistics*. Translated by Mary E. Meek. Coral Gables, Fla.: Univ. of Miami Press, 1971.

Bjornson, Richard. "*Guzmán de Alfarache*: Apologia for a 'Converso.'" *Romanische Forschungen* 85 (1973):314–29.

———. *The Picaresque Hero in European Fiction*. Madison: Univ. of Wisconsin Press, 1977.

Blanco Aguinaga, Carlos. "Cervantes y la picaresca. Notas sobre dos tipos de realismo." *Nueva Revista de Filología Hispánica* 11 (1957):313–42.

Bleiberg, Germán. *El "Informe secreto" de Mateo Alemán sobre el trabajo forzoso en las minas de Almadén*. London: Tamesis, 1985.

———. "Mateo Alemán y los galeotes." *Revista de Occidente* 39, no. 4 (1976):330–63.

Brancaforte, Benito, ed. *Guzmán de Alfarache*, by Mateo Alemán. Madrid: Cátedra, 1979.

———. "Guzmán de Alfarache: Juez-penitente." In *Aspetti e problemi delle letterature iberiche: studi offerti a Franco Meregalli*, edited by Giuseppe Bellini, 61–78. Rome: Bulzoni, 1981.

———. *Guzmán de Alfarache: ¿Conversión o proceso de degradación?*. Madison: Univ. of Wisconsin Press, 1980.

Bruss, Elizabeth. *Autobiographical Acts*. Baltimore: Johns Hopkins Univ. Press, 1976.

Cañedo, Jesús. "El 'curriculum vitae' del pícaro." *Revista de Filología Española* 49 (1976):125–80.

Carey, Douglas M. "*Lazarillo de Tormes* and the Quest for Authority." *PMLA* 94, no. 1 (1979):36–46.

Carrillo, Francisco. *Semiolingüística de la novela picaresca*. Madrid: Cátedra, 1982.

———. "*La vida del pícaro (1601)*: Testimonio contextual de la picaresca." In *Actas del Octavo Congreso de la Asociación Internacional de Hispanistas*, edited by Kossoff, Amor y Vázquez, Kossoff, and Ribbans, vol. 1, 357–66. Madrid: Istmo, 1986.

Cascardi, Anthony. "The Rhetoric of Defense in the *Guzmán de Alfarache*." *Neophilologus* 63 (1979):380–88.

Castro, Américo. *De la edad conflictiva*. Madrid: Taurus, 1971.

———. "Perspectiva de la novela picaresca." In *Hacia Cervantes*. 1957. Reprint. Madrid: Taurus, 1977.

Cavillac, Michel. *Gueux et marchands dans* Le Guzmán de Alfarache *(1599–1604). Roman picaresque et mentalité bourgeoise dans l'Espagne du Siécle d'Or*. Bordeaux: Univ. de Bordeaux, 1982.

Chandler, Frank Wadleigh. *The Literature of Roguery*. 2 vols. Cambridge, Mass.: Riverdale Press, 1907.

Chevalier, Maxime. "*Guzmán de Alfarache* en 1605: Mateo Alemán frente a su público." *Anuario de letras* 11 (1973):125–47.

Cortázar, Celina S. de. "Notas para el estudio de la estructura de *Guzmán de Alfarache* de Mateo Alemán." *Filología* 8 (1972):79–95.

Croll, Morris W. "The Baroque Style in Prose." In *Seventeenth-Century Prose: Modern Essays in Criticism*, edited by Stanley Fish, 26–52. New York: Oxford Univ. Press, 1971.

Cros, Edmond. "Deux épîtres inédites de Mateo Alemán." *Bulletin Hispanique i* 67 (1975):334–36.

———. *Mateo Alemán: Introducción a su vida y a su obra*. Salamanca: Anaya, 1971.

———. "Prédication carcérale et structure de textes." *Litterature* 36 (1979):61–74.

———. *Protée et le gueux, Recherches sur les origines et la nature du récit picaresque dans* Guzmán de Alfarache. Paris: Didier, 1977.

———. *Theory and Practice of Sociocriticism*. Translated by Jerome Schwartz. Foreward by Jurgen Link and Ursula Link-Heer. Theory and History of Literature, vol. 53. Minneapolis: Univ. of Minnesota Press, 1988.

———. "La vie de Mateo Alemán: Quelques documents inédits. Quelques suggestions." *Bulletin Hispanique i* 72 (1970):331–37.

Cruickshank, D. W. "Literature and the Booktrade in Golden Age Spain." *Modern Language Review* 73 (1978):799–824.

Davis, Barbara. "The Style of Mateo Alemán's *Guzmán de Alfarache*." *Romanic Review* 66 (1975):199–213.

Davis, Nina Cox. "Confidence and the *corullero*: *Guzmán de Alfarache*." In *Conflicts of Discourse, Spanish Literature of the Golden Age*, edited by P. W. Evans, 48–68. Manchester, England: Manchester Univ. Press, 1990.

———. "Guzmán('s) Swindles." *Symposium* 43, no. 3 (1989):194–208.

———. "Indigestion and Edification in the *Guzmán de Alfarache*." *Modern Language Notes* 104, no. 2 (1989):304–14.

———. "The *Pícaro* as Jester in the Spanish Picaresque." *Romance Quarterly* 36, no. 1 (1989):49–61.

del Monte, Alberto. *Itinerario de la novela picaresca española*. Translated by Enrique Sordo. Barcelona: Lumen, 1971.

Deleito y Piñuela, José. *El rey se divierte*. Madrid: Espasa-Calpe, 1955.

Delgado Gómez, Angel. "La autobiografía y la segunda persona: El lector del *Guzmán de Alfarache*." *Revista Chilena de Literatura* 27–28 (1986):77–91.

Dunn, Peter N. "Cervantes De/reconstructs the Picaresque." *Cervantes* 2 (1982): 109–31.

———. *The Spanish Picaresque Novel*. Boston: Twayne, 1979.

Elbaz, Robert. *The Changing Nature of Self: A Critical Study of the Autobiographic Discourse*. Iowa City: Univ. of Iowa Press, 1987.

Eoff, Sherman. "The Picaresque Psychology of Guzmán de Alfarache." *Hispanic Review* 21 (1953):107–19.

Fish, Stanley. *Self-Consuming Artifacts: The Experience of Seventeenth-Century Literature*. Berkeley: Univ. of California Press, 1972.

Folkenflik, Vivian. "Vision and Truth: Baroque Art Metaphors in *Guzmán de Alfarache*." *Modern Language Notes* 88 (1973):347–55.

Foucault, Michel. *The Archeology of Knowledge*. Translated by A. M. Sheridan Smith. New York: Pantheon, 1972.

———. *Discipline and Punish: The Birth of the Prison*. Translated by Alan Sheridan. New York: Pantheon, 1977.

Friedman, Edward H. "The Picaresque as Autobiography." In *Autobiography in Early Modern Spain*, edited by Nicholas Spadaccini and Jenaro Talens, 119–27. Minneapolis: Univ. of Minnesota Press, 1988.

Genette, Gérard. *Figures*. Vol. 2–3. Paris: Editions du Seuil, 1976.

———. *Narrative Discourse: An Essay in Method*. Translated by Jane E. Lewin. Ithaca: Cornell Univ. Press, 1980.

Godzich, Wlad, and Nicholas Spadaccini. "Popular Culture and Spanish Literary History." In *Literature Among Discourses: The Spanish Golden Age*, edited by Wlad Godzich and Nicholas Spadaccini, 41–61. Minneapolis: Univ. of Minnesota Press, 1986.

González Echevarría, Roberto. "The Life and Adventures of Cipión: Cervantes and the Picaresque." *Diacritics* 10, no. 3 (1980):15–26.

Gracián Dantisco, Lucas. *Galateo español*. Edited by Margherita Morreale. Madrid: Consejo Superior de Investigaciones Científicas, 1978.

Gracián, Baltasar. *Agudeza y arte de ingenio*. In *Obras completas*, edited by Arturo del Hoyo. 3d ed. Madrid: Aguilar, 1971.

———. *El criticón*. In *Obras completas*, edited by Arturo del Hoyo. 3d ed. Madrid: Aguilar, 1971.

Green, Otis. "On the Attitude Toward the *vulgo* in the Spanish *Siglo de Oro*." *Studies in the Renaissance* 4 (1957):190–200.

Greenblatt, Stephen, ed. *Representing the English Renaissance*. Berkeley: Univ. of California Press, 1988.

———. "Improvisation and Power." In *Literature and Society*, edited by Edward W. Said, 57–99. Baltimore: Johns Hopkins Univ. Press, 1980.

---. *Renaissance Self-Fashioning: From More to Shakespeare*. Chicago: Univ. of Chicago Press, 1980.

Guerreiro, Henri. "Guzmán y el cocinero o del estilo de servir a príncipes. Breve cala y cata en el parasitismo del mundo aristocrático." *Criticón* 28 (1984):137–39.

---. "Honra, jerarquía social y pesimismo en la obra de Mateo Alemán." *Criticón* 25 (1984):115–82.

---. "A propos des origines de Guzmán: Le determinism en question." *Criticón* 9 (1980):103–69.

Guillén, Claudio. *Literature as System*. Princeton: Princeton Univ. Press, 1971.

---. "Los pleitos extremeños de Mateo Alemán: 1. El juez, 'Dios de la tierra.'" *Archivo Hispalense* 33 (1970):387–407.

Herrero, Miguel. "Nueva interpretación de la novela picaresca." *Revista de Filología Española* 24 (1937):343–62.

Howarth, William L. "Some Principles of Autobiography." *New Literary History* 5 (1973–74):363–81.

Ife, B. W. *Reading and Fiction in Golden-Age Spain: A Platonist Critique and Some Picaresque Replies*. Cambridge: Cambridge Univ. Press, 1985.

Johnson, Carroll. *Inside Guzmán de Alfarache*. Berkeley: Univ. of California Press, 1978.

Joly, Monique. *La Bourle et son interprétation. Recherches sur le passage de la facétie au roman (Espagne, XVIe–XVIIe siècles)*. Atelier National, Reproduction des Theses, Universite Lille. Toulouse: Iberie Recherche, Universite de Toulouse, 1982.

Jones, J. A. "The Duality and Complexity of the *Guzmán de Alfarache*." In *Knaves and Swindlers*, edited by Christine Whitbourn, 25–47. London: Oxford Univ. Press, 1974.

Lapesa, Rafael. *Historia de la lengua española*. 8th ed. Madrid: Gredos, 1980.

Laurenti, Joseph L. *Bibliografía de la literatura picaresca: Suplemento*. New York: AMS Press, 1981.

---. *Bibliografía de la literatura picaresca*. Metuchen, N. J.: Scarecrow Press, 1973.

---. *Los prólogos en las novelas picarescas españolas*. Madrid: Castalia, 1971.

Lejeune, Philippe. *Le Pacte autobiographique*. Paris: Editions du Seuil, 1975.

Longhurst, C. A. "The Problems of Conversion and Repentance in *Guzmán de Alfarache*." In *A Face not Turned to the Wall: Essays on Hispanic Themes for Gareth Alban*, edited by C. A. Longhurst, 85–110. Leeds: Univ. of Leeds Press, 1987.

McGrady, Donald. *Mateo Alemán*. New York: Twayne, 1978.

Maravall, José Antonio. "From the Renaissance to the Baroque: The Diphasic Schema of a Social Crisis." Translated by Terry Cochran. In *Literature Among Discourses: The Spanish Golden Age*, edited by Wlad Godzich and Nicholas Spadaccini, 3–40. Minneapolis: Univ. of Minnesota Press, 1986.

---. *La literatura picaresca desde la historia social*. Madrid: Taurus, 1986.

---. "Relaciones de dependencia e integración social: Criados, graciosos y pícaros." *Ideologies and Literature* 1, no. 4 (1977):3–32.

Marin, Louis. "On the Theory of Written Enunciation: The Notion of Interruption-Resumption in Autobiography." *Semiotica*, suppl. (1981):101–11.

Michaud, Monique. *Mateo Alemán, Moraliste Chrétien. De L'Apologue Picaresque a L'Apologétique Tridentine*. Paris: Aux Amateurs de Livres, 1987.

Miller, Stuart. *The Picaresque Novel.* Cleveland: Case Western Reserve Univ. Press, 1977.

Molho, Maurice. *Introducción al pensamiento picaresco.* Translated by Augusto Gálvez-Cañero y Pidal. Madrid: Anaya, 1972.

Moreno Báez, Enrique. *Lección y sentido del* Guzmán de Alfarache. Madrid: Consejo Superior de Investigaciones Científicas, 1948.

Nagy, Edward. "El anhelo de Guzmán de Alfarache de 'conocer su sangre,' una posibilidad interpretativa." *Kentucky Romance Quarterly* 16 (1970):75–95.

Norval, M. N. "Original Sin and the 'conversion' in the *Guzmán de Alfarache.*" *Bulletin of Hispanic Studies* 51 (1974):346–64.

Oakley, R. J. "The Problematic Unity of the *Guzmán de Alfarache.*" In *Hispanic Studies in Honour of Joseph Manson,* edited by Dorothy M. Atkinson and Anthony H. Clarke, 185–206. Oxford: Dolphin, 1972.

Parker, A. A. *Literature and the Delinquent.* Edinburgh: Edinburgh Univ. Press, 1977.

Paulson, Ronald. "The Fool-Knave Relation in Picaresque Satire." *Rice University Studies* 51, no. 1 (1975):59–81.

Peale, C. George. "*Guzmán de Alfarache* como discurso oral." *Journal of Hispanic Philology* 4, no. 1 (1979):25–57.

Quevedo y Villegas, Francisco de. "Obras festivas." In *Obras completas,* edited by Felicidad Buendía, vol. 1, 48–59. Madrid: Aguilar, 1958.

Reed, Helen H. *The Reader in the Picaresque Novel.* London: Tamesis, 1984.

Reed, Walter L. *An Exemplary History of the Novel: The Quixotic Versus the Picaresque.* Chicago: Univ. of Chicago Press, 1981.

Renza, Louis. "The Veto of the Imagination: A Theory of Autobiography." *New Literary History* 9 (1977–78):2–26.

Rey, Alfonso. "La novela picaresca y el narrador fidedigno." *Hispanic Review* 47 (1979):55–75.

Ricapito, Joseph V., ed. *La vida de Lazarillo de Tormes y de sus fortunas y adversidades.* Madrid: Cátedra, 1983.

———. *Bibliografía razonada y anotada de las obras maestras de la picaresca española.* Madrid: Castalia, 1980.

———. "Mateo Alemán, Two Editors and the Structure of *Guzmán de Alfarache.*" *Hispanic Journal* 6, no. 1 (1984):11–19.

———. "'Tiempo Contado y Tiempo Vivido': A Study of Time in *Guzmán de Alfarache.*" In *Estudios de literatura española y francesa: Siglos XVI y XVII: Homenaje a Horst Baader,* edited by Frauke Gewecke, 149–60. Frankfurt: Klaus Dieter Vervuert, 1984.

Rico, Francisco, ed. *La novela picaresca española.* Barcelona: Planeta, 1977.

———. "Estructuras y reflejos de estructuras en el *Guzmán de Alfarache.*" *Modern Language Notes* 82, no. 2 (1977):171–84.

———. *La novela picaresca y el punto de vista.* Barcelona: Seix Barral, 1979.

———. "Para el Prólogo del *Lazarillo*: 'El deseo de alabanza.'" In *Etudes Sociocritiques: Picaresque Espagnole,* edited by Edmond Cros, 101–16. Montpellier: Actes de la Table Ronde International du CNRS, 1974.

Riggan, William. "The Reformed Picaro and His Narrative: A Study of the Autobiographical Accounts of Lucius Apuleius, Simplicius Simplicissimus, Lazarillo de Tormes, Guzmán de Alfarache, and Moll Flanders." *Orbis Litterarum* 30 (1975): 165–86.

Riley, E. C. *Cervantes's Theory of the Novel.* Oxford: Oxford Univ. Press, 1972.

Rodríguez Marín, Francisco. *Documentos referentes a Mateo Alemán y sus deudos más cercanos.* Madrid: Archivos, 1933.

Rodríguez, Carlos A. "Guzmán de Alfarache, narrador: La poética del gracioso." *Kentucky Romance Quarterly* 31 (1984):403–12.

———. *El narrador pícaro: Guzmán de Alfarache.* Madison: Seminary of Medieval Studies, 1985.

Russell, P. E. "English Seventeenth-Century Interpretations of Spanish Literature." *Atlante* 1, no. 2 (1953):65–77.

Salillas, Rafael. *Hampa (antropología picaresca): el delincuente español.* Madrid: Suárez, 1898.

San Miguel, Angel. *Sentido y estructura del* Guzmán de Alfarache. Madrid: Gredos, 1971.

Shipley, George. "The Critic as Witness for the Prosecution: Making the Case Against Lázaro de Tormes." *PMLA* 97 (March 1982):179–94.

———. "Lazarillo de Tormes Was Not a Hardworking, Clean-living Water Carrier." In *Hispanic Studies in Honor of Alan D. Deyermond: A North American Tribute*, edited by John S. Miletich, 247–55. Madison: Hispanic Seminary, 1986.

Sicroff, A. A. "Américo Castro and His Critics: Eugenio Asensio." *Hispanic Review* 40 (1972):1–30.

Sieber, Harry. *Language and Society in* La Vida de Lazarillo de Tormes. Baltimore: Johns Hopkins Univ. Press, 1978.

Silverman, Joseph H. "Some Aspects of Literature and Life in the Golden Age of Spain." In *Estudios de literatura española ofrecidos a Marcos A. Morínigo*, 133–70. Madrid: Insula, 1971.

Smith, Hilary. "The *Pícaro* Turns Preacher: Guzmán de Alfarache's Missed Vocation." *Forum for Modern Language Studies* 14 (1978):387–97.

Smith, Paul Julian. *Writing in the Margin: Spanish Literature of the Golden Age.* Oxford: Clarendon Press, 1988.

Sobejano, Gonzalo. "De Alemán a Cervantes: Monólogo y diálogo." In *Homenaje al Profesor Muñoz Cortés*, 713–29. Murcia: Univ. de Murcia, 1977.

———. "De la intención y valor del *Guzmán de Alfarache.*" *Romanische Forschungen* 71 (1959):267–311.

———. "Un perfil de la picaresca: El pícaro hablador." In *Studia hispánica in honorem R. Lapesa*, vol. 3, 467–85. Madrid: Cátedra, 1972.

Valbuena Prat, Angel. *La novela picaresca española.* Madrid: Aguilar, 1943.

van Praag, J. A. "Sobre el sentido del *Guzmán de Alfarache.*" In *Estudios dedicados a Menéndez Pidal*, vol. 5, 283–306. Madrid: Consejo Superior de Investigaciones Científicas, 1954.

Whitenack, Judith A. *The Impenitent Confession of Guzmán de Alfarache.* Madison: Seminary of Medieval Studies, 1985.

Woods, Madison J. "The Teasing Opening of the *Guzmán de Alfarache.*" *Bulletin of Hispanic Studies* 57 (1980):213–18.

Woodward, L. J. "*El casamiento engañoso y el Coloquio de los perros.*" *Bulletin of Hispanic Studies* 36 (1959):80–87.

Zahareas, Anthony N. "The Historical Function of Picaresque Autobiographies: Toward a History of Social Offenders." In *Autobiography in Early Modern Spain*, edited by Nicholas Spadaccini and Jenaro Talens, 129–62. Minneapolis: Univ. of Minnesota Press, 1988.

Zarandieta Mirabent, E. *El "golfo" en la novela picaresca y el "golfo" en Madrid.* Madrid: J. Ratés, 1916.

Index

agudeza, types of, 109
Agüera, Victorio, 134n.6
Arias, Joan, 20, 47, 134n.6, 136n.29, 137n.34, 142n.11
Asensio, Eugenio, 134n.6
atalaya, 45, 47
autobiography: as linguistic act, 18–19, 61, 129–31; as fiction, 19–20, 23–24, 26, 61; theory of, 19–20, 23–24, 108, 134n.8, 134n.9. *See* Picaresque autobiographies
Ayala, Francisco, 137n.34
Babcock, Barbara, 142n.7
Bakhtin, Mikhail, 136n.32, 139n.10
Barros, Alonso de, 24, 26, 27, 41, 42–43, 47, 49, 55, 62
Barthes, Roland, 108
Bataillón, Marcel, 134n.6
Benveniste, Emile, 19, 20, 108, 132n.2, 133n.11
Bjornson, Richard, 134n.6
Blanco Aguinaga, Carlos, 133n.5, 138n.5
Bleiberg, Germán, 135n.15
Brancaforte, Benito, 21, 43, 46-47, 98, 104, 134n.6, 135n.20, 136n.27
Bruss, Elizabeth, 134n.8
burlador burlado, 58–59, 87
burlador indiscreto, definition of, 17, 91–93. *See* joker.
burlas: definitions of, 14, 61, 63, 130–31, 132n.6, 138n.2; *burlas pesadas*, 67, 140n.20; "deceiving with the truth" as a class of *burlas*, 69, 92, 111, 121, 125; critical studies of *burlas* in the *Guzmán*, 14–18. *See* Chevalier; Joly; Rodríguez.
Cañedo, Jesús, 140n.17
Carey, Douglas, 135n.17
carnivalesque metaphors and their function: alimentary and digestive, 65–66, 70–72, 73–77, 83–91

Carrillo, Francisco, 133n.10,
Cascardi, Anthony, 44
Castro, Américo, 134n.6, 135–36n.24, 136n.29
Cavillac, Michel, 134n.7
Chandler, Frank, 22, 133n.4
Chevalier, Maxime, 14
chocarrero, 137n.40
Cortázar, Celina, 125, 142n.9
corulla, 103–4. *See also* discourse: nautical discourse
corullero, 99, *See also corulla*
criminality: in the picaresque, 24; in the *Guzmán*, 28–29, 39–40, 44, 47, 50–52. *See* Cascardi, Zahareas
Croll, Morris, 142n.6
Cros, Edmond, 35, 46, 98, 134n.7, 135n.15
Cruickshank, D.W., 135n.16
Davis, Barbara, 35, 135n.20, 143n.14
Davis, Nina, 137n.41, 139n.14, 141n.28, 142n.8
del Monte, Alberto, 134n.6
Deleito y Piñuela, 137n.39
Delgado Gómez, Angel, 135n.11
discourse in the *Guzmán*: critical debate over its monologic versus heteroglossic message, 13, 22, 133–34n.5, 134n.6; dialogism of the narration, 20, 25, 134–35n.11; plural points of view in one voice, 45–47, 58; sermonic discourse, 38–41, 104–5, 119–21; mercantile discourse, 104–5, 114–15, 117–18, 122–23; judicial discourse, 39–40, 118–19; nautical discourse, 96, 99, 141n.26. *See also* narration, religious conversion, Cros, Delgado Gómez, Longhurst, Peale, P. Smith, Sobejano

152 INDEX

discretos: definitions of, 17, 133n.9; as recipients of *burlas*, 66–67; 78–79, 81–82, 84–85, 103
Dunn, Peter, 133–34n.5
Elbaz, Robert, 23–24, 134n.8
engaño: defined, 58–59; exemplified in narration of swindles, 112–16, 116–21, 121–26
Eoff, Sherman, 67, 138n.8, 140n.18
figura, definition of, 19, 25, 41–43, 55, 62, 110, 136n.26
Fish, Stanley, 142n.6
Folkenflik, Vivian, 136n.31
Foucault, Michel, 45, 136n.32
Friedman, Edward, 19–20, 137n.34
Genette, Gerard, 109, 142n.5
Godzich, Wlad, 141n.4
González Echevarría, Roberto, 138n.3
Gracián Dantisco, Lucas, 138n.2, 140–41n.25
Gracián, Baltasar, 141n.3
gracioso, 91, 137n.40. *See burlador indiscreto*
Green, Otis, 135n.16
Greenblatt, Stephen, 42, 136n.25
Guerreiro, Henri, 134n.7, 136n.28, 139n.14
Guillén, Claudio, 133n.1
Guzmán de Alfarache, reception of: as bestseller, 22, 133n.1; dedicated to courtier patronage, 28, 30–32; authorial designation of readers by levels, as *discretos lectores*, 27, 32, 34–36, 42–43, 52, 54–60; and as the *vulgo*, 27, 31–32, 33–35, 42–43; problems of distinguishing levels, 62–63
Herrero, Miguel, 133n.5
honor: definitions of, 44–45, 64, 66–67, 68, 83, 124–25, 126–27, 130–31, 136n.29
Howarth, William, 134n.9
Ife, B.W., 32, 67, 109, 133n.12
jester, definition of, 17. *See juglar discreto*
Johnson, Carroll, 22–23, 134n.6, 142–43n.12
joker, definition of, 17. *See burlador indiscreto*
Joly, Monique, 14–15, 17, 62, 70, 140 nn.20, 23
Jones, J.A., 136n.30
juglar discreto, definition of, 17, 69, 79–91, 137n.40 *See* jester.

Lapesa, Rafael, 118
Laurenti, Joseph, 133n.1, 135n.13
Lazarillo de Tormes: echoes of in lexicon of *Guzmán*, 27, 29, 30, 33, 36–38, 102, 135n.17, 138n.7; polysemia of, 135 n.22; terms cited in study, 135n.23; as model for narrative temporal sequencing, 95–97
Lejeune, Philippe, 134n.8
Longhurst, C.A., 40, 141n.29. *See* religious conversion
Mabbe, James, 132nn.4, 7, 133n.2
Maravall, José Antonio, 16, 132n.8, 138 nn.4, 6
Marin, Louis, 141n.2
Martí, Juan, 43, 50, 137n.36
McGrady, Donald, 133n.5, 135n.15, 136 n.30, 137n.38
Michaud, Monique, 134n.5
Miller, Stuart, 135–36n.24
Molho, Maurice, 134n.7
Moreno Báez, Enrique, 98, 133n.5
Nagy, Edward, 134n.6
narration: function as discourse, 20, 108–11; the control of its monologic form, 61, 127–28. *See also* Barthes, Benveniste, temporal planes
narrative: function as history/story, 20; its exemplarity, 61–62, 109–11; as representation of the process of narration, 127–28. *See also* Barthes, Benveniste, temporal planes
Norval, M.N., 134n.6
Oakley, R.J., 140n.23
Parker, A.A., 98, 133n.5, 136n.30
Paulson, Ronald, 136–37n.33
Peale, C. George, 135n.11, 136n.30
picaresque autobiographies: historical function of, 24, 26, 27–28, 129–31. *See* Zahareas
pícaro: definition of, 13; literary function of, 16–18, 23, 27–28, 48, 53, 129–31. *See* Barros, *figura*
prologues: function of dual format in *Guzmán*, 32–33; prologue to the *vulgo*, 33–35; prologue to the *discreto lector*, 35–36; comparison with prologue of the *Lazarillo*, 36–38; subversion of distinction between classes of readers, 62–63. *See Guzmán de Alfarache*: reception of

Quevedo y Villegas, Francisco de, 136 n.26
Reed, Helen, 15, 19, 25, 27, 33, 34, 35, 111
Reed, Walter, 136n.33
religious conversion, 97, 98, 103–4, 104–5. *See* Longhurst, Whitenack, Ricapito
Renza, Louis, 24
Rey, Alfonso, 136n.30
Ricapito, Joseph, 36, 97, 133n.1, 138n.1
Rico, Francisco, 14, 21, 98, 118, 132n.1, 132–33n.8, 133–34nn.5, 12, 135n.22, 136 n.30, 138n.5, 140n.24
Riggan, William, 136n.31
Riley, E.C., 135nn.16, 18
Rodgríguez Marín, Francisco, 135n.14
Rodríguez, Carlos, 14, 16, 17–18, 53, 59, 134n.6
Russell, P.E., 134n.5
Salillas, Rafael, 133n.4
San Miguel, Angel, 117, 136n.29, 140 n.17, 142nn.9, 11
Shipley, George, 135n.17
Sicroff, A.A., 134n.6
Sieber, Harry, 18, 135n.17
Silverman, Joseph, 134n.6
Smith, Hilary, 137n.35
Smith, Paul Julian, 13, 23, 26, 45–46
Sobejano, Gonzalo, 23, 24, 25, 29, 33, 134n.10, 140n.21
sociocriticism: analyses of the Spanish picaresque, 13, 134n.7
Spadaccini, Nicholas, 141–42n.4
subjectivity: produced by linguistic shifters, 19
temporal planes: Benveniste's *histoire* and *discours* translated, 20; discussion of their relationship in the *Guzmán*, 21, 108, 127–28, 132n.2, 133n.12. *See also* Benveniste, Ife, narration, narrative
Valbuena Prat, Angel, 133–34n.5
van Praag, J.A., 134n.6
vulgo: definitions of, 17; as recipients of *burlas*, 67–68, 73–75, 81–82
Whitenack, Judith, 134n.6
Woods, Madison, 44
Woodward, L.J., 140n.22
Zahareas, Anthony, 24
Zarandieta Mirabent, E., 133n.4